What Happens on Page 27?

Tested oral exercises and poetry
prompts for classroom and home

By Emmanuel Williams

ISBN-10: 1544708009

ISBN-13: 978-1544708003

Cover art: from a drawing by Serafina Manferrari
Cover design: Davina Williams
Layout: Davina Williams

Reviews for *What Happens on Page 27?*

"Emmanuel Williams understands the essence of how schools should foster creativity with students of all ages. In <u>What Happens on Page 27?</u> Williams presents his knowledgeable approach to writing and helping even the most reluctant writers find their voices."

> *- Ashley McCrae, Elementary School Teacher*

"In *What Happens on Page 27?*, Williams offers way upon way of engaging the right brain, unleashing creativity, turning writing into fascination and fun. His ideas are little fuses: light them in your classroom and watch imagination explode. This book is genius and will draw genius from children – and adults – anywhere."

> *- Catherine Elizabeth Dana, Teacher of Creative Expressions and Creative Writing at Alameda Community Learning Center and Author of My Dad Believed in Love*

"Emmanuel Williams has created a book that should be on the bookshelf of every dedicated teacher and group facilitator. These ideas work for all ages (8yrs - 80+).

- for college level trades classes to create class comfort, humour and the use of creative problem solving
- in seniors activity gatherings to promote brain activity, verbal exchanges, community fun and a possible 'take home' product
- for math classes to promote 'thinking outside the box', cooperative learning, and comfort between students
- for drama warm ups, creating class plays, etc
- and for a series of language arts activities at all levels with a productive outcome
- for substitute teachers to establish a relaxed and productive atmosphere in a strange classroom
- for making use of those empty few minutes of classroom 'waiting'
- for preschoolers - language development and fluidity

Williams' introduction gives a well-researched rationale for the use of right brain activities. As a teacher I know activities like these are what makes students want to come to school – they learn so much without even being aware of it. His book provides a thorough explanation of a wide range of exceptional, well organised exercises that can be used with little preparation, and in any order. I will take this book into the classroom to help me build class management, student success, and a friendly intergroup supportive atmosphere."

> *- Elfridah Schagen, Middle School Teacher - emphasis on drama and art*

"Emmanuel Williams' book is both an inspiration and a practical, down-to-earth source of ideas. I've used it to create a poetry unit and it has allowed my students, who have had very little exposure to poetry prior to this class, to become poets in their own right. They have even submitted anthologies with the poems they created using p. 27 and the lessons and ideas in the book. Their poems are beautiful and they are so proud of them!"

- Rosabelle Lynes, High School English teacher

"Emmanuel Williams has written a joyful and practical handbook for teachers everywhere. In his Introduction, he makes reasoned and well-researched arguments for including even small amounts of creative writing in our classrooms, highlighting the need to exercise all sides of our students' brains if we want them to develop as full human beings. As a former Statewide Director of the California Poets In The Schools program and an English and writing teacher for over thirty years, I'm impressed by the richness and abundance of imaginative activities in his new book. I want to find a group of students and try his interview exercise today. I want to call my friends who work in the Poets In The Schools program and show them Emmanuel's counting poems activity. And I want to tell my hard-working teacher colleagues in K-12 classrooms about "thinking crazy or sideways" as a way to liven up their students' writing. There are so many original and exciting activities here. In a perfect world, every classroom teacher would receive a free copy of *What Happens On Page 27?* by Emmanuel Williams. Let it be so!"

- Katharine Harer, English & Creative Writing Professor

"I had the privilege of hosting Mr. Williams in my seventh-grade classroom wherein he personally presented numerous activities from this book. My students couldn't get enough. They were so proud of their own resulting creations--and themselves. They were in awe of their creativity and were inspired to continue. As a result, I use the activities from this book as often as time can afford because I feel it is vital to students to feel like they are innovative. The pathways that these activities open in students' minds are both astounding and heartwarming--and it sure takes the pressure off of us teachers to reinvent the wheel."

- Tiffany Woods, Middle School Teacher

This book is dedicated to all the students
I have worked with over the years.

CONTENTS

PROLOGUE

Two Intelligences

There are two kinds of intelligence:
one is acquired,
as when a student memorizes facts and concepts from books
from what the teacher says
from literature, from science,
from the procedures and patterns of mathematics.

With such intelligence you rise in the world.
You are graded, tested, ranked before or behind others
according to your competence
in retaining information.
You go on and on
with this intelligence
in and out of fields of knowledge
always accumulating more and more marks
in the files with your name on them.

There is yet another kind
of intelligence. It is complete
already and alive inside you. It is like
a spring flowing from some deep source. It is
a freshness in the center of the chest.
This other intelligence
does not turn yellow or stagnate. It's fluid,
and it doesn't move from outside to inside,
through the blueprint plumbing
of learning conduits.
This second knowing is a fountainhead
flowing from within you
out into the world.

– Rumi

INTRODUCTION

"The wealth of nations and the well-being of individuals now depend on having artists in the room."
– Daniel Pink

There's a story told about a man named Gordon Mackenzie, long-time designer for Hallmark Cards. When he visited schools to talk about his work he'd introduce himself as an artist. He'd then ask the children to raise their hands if they were artists. The answers invariably followed a similar pattern: in kindergarten and first grade classes, every hand went up. In second grade it was about three quarters of the hands, in third grade a few, and by sixth grade no hands at all were raised.

This story points to a great loss, one that affects not just young people, but of all of us.

"...the whole system of public education around the world is a protracted process of university entrance. And the consequence is that many highly talented, brilliant, creative people think they're not, because the thing they were good at school wasn't valued, or was actually stigmatized. And I think we can't afford to go on that way."

– Sir Ken Robinson

(You can watch the whole speech on www.ted.com)

Schools should not only teach knowledge and skills, but also help young people develop their creativity. Most schools – and I visit lots of them – aren't doing this. Consequently children and young people are growing up lopsidedly – big left brains, small right brains. What can be done about this? There are many excellent critiques of education, and visions of how our schools should be re-organised, or re-imagined. Unfortunately education systems are like huge cargo ships; they take a long time to make significant changes of direction. The current academically-based mode will probably persist for another decade, so change must come from the bottom up. I believe it's up to the classroom teacher to give time and space to creativity. Which, I acknowledge, is hard. Most teachers are over-worked, and – especially at the high school level – struggling to cope with too many students.

We tend to assume that it must be one or the other – that we either cover the prescribed curriculum, or we turn classrooms into creative arts labs. "*In the U.S. today we have created a bogus opposition between arts learning and other kinds of learning,*" says National Endowment of the Art's Dana Gioia, noting that virtually every week he learns of another school district that has canceled arts programs to focus on other areas of study. "*This strikes me as a recipe for disaster. There is an enormous amount of research still to be done, but I think we know enough today to say that education policy and budget makers are using a false model... The purpose of education is to realize the full potential of each child. To do that, children need exposure to a broad range of arts training, not just traditional hard academic subjects.*"

It doesn't have to be one or the other. There's plenty of evidence to show that students frequently exposed to the arts and to creative activities do better in basic and academic subjects. An evaluation of California Poets In The Schools poets conducted in 2000 – 2003 showed some impressively positive results which included: "*Creative work, because it is personal, self-generated or proactive, and is outside the right/wrong continuum, nourishes self-esteem significantly.*" A 2009 report entitled "Staying in school: Arts Education and NYC High

School Graduation Rates" offers conclusive evidence that "*...the arts play a key role in keeping students in high school and graduating on time*" (https://centerforartsed.org/).

Why is this? Maybe it's because when a student writes a poem that "works" – one that elicits a genuinely positive response from his or her peers and that he or she is pleased with – then that student's sense of satisfaction is probably greater than that derived from a high score in – for example – a spelling test. Success in creativity is success on one's own terms. It's proactive. "*I wrote that! I thought that up! It all comes from me!*"

In addition to the issue of the overall balanced development of our students, there's another rationale for creative, or right brain, work which has to do with major socio-economic changes in the world, a topic well covered by Daniel Pink in his book: "The Whole New Mind." Mr. Pink's central thesis is that left-brained tasks are increasingly being taken over by machines, robots and automation, or out–sourced to trained technicians and left-brain workers in India, Russia and China. He writes: "*If standardized routine left-brain directed work can be done for a lot less overseas and delivered to clients instantly via optic links, that's where the work will go.*" This being so, the Western nations and Japan must respond with an emphasis on the right brain or what Pink calls: "High concept, high touch".

"*We need to supplement our well-developed high-tech abilities with abilities that are also high concept and high touch...high concept involves the ability to create artistic and emotional beauty, to detect patterns and opportunities, to craft a satisfying narrative and to combine seemingly unrelated ideas into a novel invention. High touch involves the ability to empathize, to understand the subtleties of human interaction, to find joy in oneself and elicit it to others, and to stretch beyond the quotidian, in pursuit of meaning and purpose"* (Whole New Mind, p. 51).

This is what's happening on the global stage beyond our classroom doors. It behooves us as teachers to be aware of these major changes and to respond to them in our work with children and young people. Otherwise we're teaching skills and habits of thought that are a lot less relevant then they were last century.

If you agree that creativity belongs in the classroom, you may benefit from a collection of practical ideas to dip into. Hence this book. Its emphasis is on language activities because they're what I'm best at. I've worked hard and sought input from other teachers to make this book as accessible and practical as possible. I've assumed that you're as busy as most of the teachers I meet, so I've included not only specific teaching ideas but a great deal of supporting material for those ideas. I've even included rough transcriptions of what I say when introducing an activity.

SECTION ONE

What Happens on Page 27?

WHY POETRY?

"There exists in every man a young dead poet, whom the man survives."

- Sainte-Beuve

There are lots of poetry writing ideas in this book. The emphasis, however, is on poetry as a medium for creativity rather than as an exercise in literary form. Here are some arguments in favor of poetry writing in the classroom:

1. It's a great way to exercise creativity simply and inexpensively. All you need is pen and paper. And you can write a poem, get some peer feedback, edit and read it aloud all in the space of a single period.

2. It's natural. Before we stop them doing it, kids think spontaneously in terms of metaphor. They play with language. They make up new words, put words together:

    "I love to watch the tall big trees in the wind-blow..."
    "The big waves are loudy loudy."

Humans have always done this. Poetry isn't literary; it's human song.

3. Poetry writing helps us discover our "voice". It reveals depths that normally go unrecognized. *"My imagination/is as long/as the path to the light..."* wrote a 6th grade girl. Writing poems, like any creative endeavor, enhances our sense of who we are.

4. When we care about what we're writing, there's no gap between life and language. It's *real.* The words are real because what they're expressing is real.

WHY *WRITE* POETRY?

When I first meet with a class I often ask students what they think the purpose of writing poetry might be. Someone usually says something like:

"It helps us express our feelings."

"Yes, good. Feelings. What else does writing poetry bring to life?" I might quote a nursery rhyme:

> *"Hey diddle diddle, the cat and the fiddle*
> *The cow jumped over the moon*
> *The little dog laughed to see such fun*
> *And the dish ran away with the spoon."*

Someone says "*imagination*" or "*creativity*".

"Yes, good. Now, as you may know, we have two sides, or hemispheres, to our brains – left and right. Does anyone know anything about these two sides of the brain - left and right?"

Quite often a hand goes up, and we explore what the right brain does, and the left brain.

Left Brain	Right Brain
Logical, sequential	Random
Rational	Intuitive
Analytical	Holistic, synthesizing
Objective	Subjective
Looks at parts	Looks at wholes

"What you do in schools... is it mainly left or right brain?"

"Left"

"What happens to any part of our bodies but we don't use very much?"

"It doesn't grow strong?"

"Right. In a way you're all going around like this..."

I tilt my head sharply to the left and hold it there.

"Big left brains, small right brains. So writing poems helps you become a better writer, gives you a way to express feelings, and exercises your right brain. But let's have a quick look at the bigger picture...how the two brains work together. They need one another. When the two hemispheres work together properly, they're a team."

Example:

- The poet's right brain discovers inspiration, ideas, images, even sometimes just the sound of a poem. The poet's left brain comes up with the words, the organization of the poem and, later, the editing.

- The architect's right brain looks for beauty, for balancing straight and curving, or solid and light. The architect's left brain deals with dimensions, materials, stresses, load bearing, and building codes.

- The scientist's right brain takes intuitive leaps, inspired guesses. The scientist's left brain works with deductive reasoning, with organized experimentation and proof.

This is the rationale I give a new class, adapted to the age group I'm talking to. I also tell them that they might discover as they write that they have a talent for writing.

"Schools should help you find out what your talents are. We all have a talent, at least one, and discovering it helps give us a direction and purpose to our lives."

IN PRAISE OF THE RIGHT BRAIN

Right brain stuff is fun! It's unpredictable, spontaneous, and often playful. It brings laughter to the classroom…discovery…an energy that's different, that's light and alive. It's good to laugh in the classroom. It's good to play, to explore the unpredictable, to find unexpected connections, to tilt things back a little towards the neglected, the rich, endlessly creative right hemisphere. It's good for your students, it's good for you and ultimately it's good for the world.

The ideas in this book are not intended to be a "First you do this then you do this…" sequence. It's more of a recipe book. I've included a lot of support material, like specific lists of possible titles for writing ideas. It's up to you which activities you want to try. As someone who taught students from 2nd grade through college I've found that most of the ideas I've gathered here work with most age groups. It's up to you to decide what's likely to work with your students. I do recommend that you try writing your own poetry in response to a particular idea.

GRADING CREATIVITY

"Too many students walk through the schoolhouse door with one aim in mind: to get good grades. And all too often, the best way to reach this goal is to get with the program, avoid risks, and serve up the answers the teacher wants the way the teacher wants them. Good grades become a reward for compliance – but don't have much to do with learning."

- Daniel Pink, (Drive, p. 176)

Please don't give grades for right brain work.

After I've read a student's writing I ask, *"Are you pleased with this? What do you think of it?"* I might suggest they have a peer read it and give feedback. If there's a line or a section that doesn't sound so good I might read it aloud and ask them what they think. I also read aloud and admire lines that work. I'm trying to scale back the ultimate authority role and follow the principle of what I once heard defined as "The theory of diminishing crutches": the teacher provides two crutches to the student, puts a hand on each shoulder and tells the student which foot to put forward first...soon one crutch is removed, then the other, then one hand, and so on. Support/control/ guidance are withdrawn as and when no longer needed. In the area of creativity – as indeed in many others – we, as adults, should aim at making ourselves unnecessary.

"Making beauty has an advantage over obtaining "A" grades because others can share in the enjoyment of a beautiful product; only the self enjoys high grades."

- Jerome Kagan

A NOTE ABOUT CHOICE

The freedom to choose what one is going to do is important. It may be difficult to arrange in the classroom, but it can be done. I often give a couple of writing ideas so that students can choose which one they want to do, and have writing prompt cards on hand if they want alternative ideas. You could, for example, make cards from the story ideas in the "Round Robin" section. And I often tell students they can work with a partner if they wish.

Creativity is like any other human skill – the more we do it the better we get at it. Try to incorporate creative writing into your classroom routine on a regular basis. Ask students to bring in poems they like. Display them. Have students read them aloud. Encourage them to make anthologies of poems they like. Encourage them to learn by heart poems they like.

Lastly – and you surely know this already – it's vital that you establish an orderly atmosphere. If there are persistently disruptive students I suggest you remove them. The tension created by discipline problems is anathema to creativity. Also, when students are writing, I've found that it's good to simply sit in the front for at least some of the time in a quiet, relaxed state. I'm observing the students but I'm also consciously holding my feeling open and wide.

ACTIVITIES

The following sections contain alphabetized lists of activities. Oral, then written. I usually begin with some oral work, then go into a writing idea. Everything, I assure you, has been tried and tested. In addition, early drafts of this book were read and commented on by several teachers.

SECTION TWO

Oral Activities

Oral Activities

Focused oral activities stimulate the flow of language and strengthen the ability to think and talk on the spot, which is an important life skill.

Basic Wordplay

Keep these activities light and quick!

A. Rhyming

You may want to prepare for this with a list of words with lots of rhymes. You say a word, point to a student (or ask for volunteers) and ask for words that rhyme with it.

Six words that rhyme with beat

eat... seat... feet... neat... repeat...

One more!

cheat

Okay... Five words rhyming with education...

vacation... station... creation... hesitation... hibernation

and so on.

B. Opposites

You say a word, point to a student says its opposite or antonym. Occasionally, just to mix things up a bit, you say a word that has no opposite.

Up – down... Backwards – forwards... Intelligent – stupid...

You can use these words as poem-starters. Every line must include one of the words. Take the cold-warm list for example:

Cold frost froze his muscle cords

ice on the puddles new and thin as a playing card

backwards and forwards swings the bare tree

in the warm wind.

-E.W.

C. Word ladders

Letter by letter, one word is transformed into another. Each step must be a word. The two beginning words must have the same number of letters.

Example: from cold to warm

cold cord card ward warm

Example: from head to tail

head heal teal tall tail

Go from: **Roof to door… Dawn to dusk… Cat to dog… Mud to sky… Ball to cube… Tram to mart**

D. Words in a word

Write a longish word on the board and ask students to find 10 words in it – *in their heads* – without writing anything down! They can write their 10 words on the board when they're ready, or say them out loud when asked to.

Example: basket

1. Ask
2. Bask
3. East
4. Beast
5. Sake
6. Take
7. Tab
8. Task

9. Bet

10. Beat

11. Stab

You can follow this up by asking students to write – quickly – a poem entitled **Basket**, each line to include one of the words they thought of.

Other useful words for this exercise: **Forecast, Caterpillar, Weather, Dreams, Carpets, Mathematics.**

A variant of this game is finding a descriptive phrase in your name. For example, in mine – Emmanuel Williams – I find (ahem!):

I am a wise man

Connections

The left brain likes to classify, to put things in compartments, to separate this from that. The right brain seeks connections. In this exercise students create scenarios that connect two things that seem to have nothing to do with one another.

Example:

"Can anyone connect great white sharks and yo-yos?"
"There was this guy invented a yo-yo that you could play with underwater..."

Here's a list (you can of course swap these around in any way you like and even, just to make things more challenging, group them in threes):

Connections:

Blueberry muffins and the full moon

Whispering and mermaids

Teeth and carpet shampoo

Marshmallows and purple

Cabbages and swimming pools

Sunshine and cold steel

Falling leaves and potato chips

Pencil sharpener and eye-shadow

Toenails and cat food

Punctuation and tornadoes

Great white sharks and yo-yos

Barbie and waterfalls

Describing Paintings

"I want you to find a partner and sit opposite one another. One of you is A, the other's B. There are several piles of reproductions of paintings placed around the classroom. A goes to the nearest pile, chooses a painting that looks interesting, goes back to their place without B seeing the painting, and describes it as carefully as possible. Describe the way the painting is organized, the subject of the painting, the people or the objects that are in it, the different colors that are used, the light in the painting, and maybe the feeling of the painting. B can ask questions - for example: "You say the sky is blue... is it deep blue or a soft faded blue... are there any clouds in the sky?" And so on. B can sketch an outline of the painting on plain paper as A describes it. Finally, B asks to see the painting and gives A feedback about what was well described, what was a bit vague, and what was left out. Then B returns the painting to the pile, chooses another one, goes back and does the same thing to A."

This activity provides good practice in descriptive language. It gives students a physical stimulus for language and gets them out of their heads. I suggest you walk around eavesdropping on their descriptions and encouraging them to be as detailed as possible. You might look at the painting A's describing and ask B questions about it: *What color is the lady's hat? What creature is sitting on the gate?* You might also hold a painting up at the beginning and describe it, giving them a model. If you have any pictures big enough, put one up where everyone can see it and have the class do a group description.

I get a lot of reproductions from used books I pick up in Goodwill stores. I sometimes print them from the net – see Olga's Galleries for a rich selection. I glue the paintings on to thin card so that they can't be seen from the back. I like the fact that this exercise gives students an opportunity to look hard at great art. Sometimes I talk a little about van Gogh or Monet or Rembrandt. I think students should know a little about great painters, just as they should be familiar with one or two pieces of music by some of the great composers – Beethoven, Mozart, Bach etc. (See Ed Hirsch – "Cultural Literacy".)

As a variation on this exercise I bring in bags of objects – driftwood, seashells, pine cones, fossils and interesting stones, things I find on the beach like lost flip-flops, plastic beach spades, anything that's small and has a fairly interesting shape. Students look through a bag, choose an object, go back to their places and describe it just as they described the painting. This is not a guessing game! The point is not for B to identify the object, but to see it as clearly as possible in the mind's eye. As in the paintings exercise, when B has seen the object and given feedback, he returns it to the bag, finds another object and brings it back to describe it.

Look for ways to give students choices. Being able to choose the painting or the object to describe is a step in this direction. Sometimes I bring in both the paintings and the objects so that they can choose one or the other. Also, I look for ways to follow up this oral activity with writing exercises about paintings or objects. We'll be looking at some of these later.

Echo Speech

Like the above, echo speech is intended to get language flowing. Students sit facing one another in pairs. One is A, one is B. A speaks and B echoes everything A says. The focus is on echoing what A says as quickly and accurately as possible. I suggest you give possible topics to talk about: *this is a description of my room; this is what I see in the classroom; this is the story of a movie I saw recently; this is what happened last summer when we went on holiday*...and so on.

As Echo Speech proceeds you do "side coaching". Students follow your directives: *"Whisper!" "Slow motion!" "High speed!" "Robot style!" "Sing!" "Sadly!" "Angrily!"* and so on. Soon you call *"Change!"* at which point B speaks and A follows.

Gibberish Interpreter

Three students in chairs in a row at the front. A, B, C. Students A and C speak gibberish. Student B, the one in the middle, interprets. A and C should know what they are talking about even though they're speaking gibberish. It helps the interpreter if they make gestures as they speak.

Guidelines: gibberish should sound like a language, not like a stuck robot repeating the same sound over and over again. The interpreter is not allowed to introduce personal insults: *"He doesn't like the shape of your ears…"* because that leads to more personal insults which quickly gets boring. If a student can't get going he says, *"I'm stuck"* and goes back to his place, without shame or embarrassment. After a while you call *"Change!"*, at which point C leaves, A and B move to the left and a new person sits in the empty chair and carries on.

Play is one of the richest right-brain activities. It brings a fresh new energy into the room. Gibberish Interpreter is playing with language. Younger students love it. Teenagers, being more self-conscious, may initially find it too much of a challenge. I chivvy them, challenge them, *"If you stay in your comfort zone you stagnate!"*… even bribe them… *"Anyone who comes up to do gibberish gets a quarter!"* When the students get into the flow of the game the results are often hilarious. It helps if you, the teacher, are able to speak gibberish as an illustration.

An offshoot of this is "gibberish commercial". This is a game for two people. You give A some item – a glue stick, a water bottle, a pencil sharpener…A improvises a commercial about the object, using gestures, smiling at the camera etc. B interprets, also using gestures and smiling happily.

Instant Similes

Similes – or, more broadly speaking, comparisons -are at their freshest and most effective when the two things being compared are very different. If you compare drizzle to standing under a cold shower, or to spray from a fountain, it's less interesting than, say, comparing drizzle to the tears of a legion of traumatized angels, or the sound of distant applause.

In this activity students are challenged to come up with a simile on the spot. You name something, say a **bagel,** and students come up with a simile for it:

a small edible frisbee with a hole in it

a giant's nose ring

a wheel from a moon buggy.

...or Spaghetti:

tangle of skinny snakes

an Italian mermaid's hair

*See page 26 for a list of simile prompters you might find useful.

Simile Prompters:

TV	Ladder	Garden hose	Donut	Umbrella
Frog	Frost	Cloud	Rainbow	Sock
Tongue	Rain	Storm	Snake	Butterfly
Skateboard	Scissors	Ice cream	Ocean	Moon
Crystal	School	Strawberry	Calendar	Camera
Mirror	Love	Traffic light	Fog	Music
Sleep	Trumpet	Baseball bat	Banana	Talent
Curtain	Mall	Driftwood	Lungs	Hair
Grass	Stars	Cell-phone	Hair dryer	Octopus
Elephant	Circus	Plough	Whale	Blister
Candle	Cave	Shooting star	Book	Navel
Snowman	Hand	White	Shadow	Eraser
Photo	Seed	Wind	Canoe	Heart
Anxiety	Skull	Pen	Drum	Acne

__Instant Symbols__

Symbols are objects or beings that stand for something beyond themselves. The cross stands for suffering, the rose for purity, the dove for peace, and so on. It makes symbols more meaningful to students if we play with them, just as we did with similes. I often introduce symbolism with the following scenario:

I walk over to the classroom door, reach out and touch it.

"Okay...we know what this is...it's a classroom door. Rectangular. Opens and closes. No prob. That's the left brain at work. Identified, classified, end of story. Now, what if I ask: What does this classroom door symbolize? What might it MEAN to you? Remember, there are NO SINGLE CORRECT ANSWERS in right brain country. There's what you come up with."

I wait. Not forcing anything.

If this is a high school classroom, what comes up may be bitter, or critical. A lot of high school students don't enjoy school. It's up to you how you deal with this.

"It's a way in."

"Okay. A way into what?"

"Prison."

"So...the classroom door symbolizes an entrance into prison."

"Okay. I understand why you say that. Anyone else? Any other meanings to the classroom door?"

"It's an opening into knowledge. A portal into a place of learning."

"Okay. Any others?"

"It's a kind of border. On one side there's the real world, with the sky, clouds, traffic, people making money, and on the other side there's this like box with books and stuff, not much movement..."

"Okay. So the classroom door is an entrance into a prison, a portal into a place of learning, a border between two worlds. All these meanings, these symbolic meanings, are equally valid."

*See page 29 & 30 for two options.

Option #1

You can do another large group symbol discussion like the above one but with a different object, or you can go straight into individual or partner work.

Symbol Prompters, Option #1

The following table contains a list of symbol prompters for the oral activity, "Instant Symbols". Choose several items, or items of your own, and give each one a possible symbolic meaning. Or more than one meaning. You can work with a partner. If you think of your own item or items, so much the better.

Bike	Skateboard	Flower	Dog
Bird	Light bulb	Milk	Tree
Car	Moon	Hoodie	Gun
Ocean	Baseball glove	Bedroom door	Music
Mountain	Tower	Tattoo	Snake
Blood	Whip	Stars	White
Glue	Heart	Skull	Hand
Mirror	Lake	Wand	River
Crab	Forest	Beach	Sandcastle
Seed	Horse	Bridge	Fog
Snow	Beard	Pig	Child
Cow	Horizon	Wall	Home

Option #2

Or, you can take a feeling and find a symbol that represents it. Shyness could be represented by a hoodie, for example. Loneliness by an empty street in the rain.

Find symbols for the following:

Symbol Prompters, Option #2			
Anger	Courage	Tenacity	Fear
Uncertainty	Love	Self-confidence	Aggression
Greed	Forgiveness	Delight	Familiarity
Lying	Strength	Honor	Sadness

Interviews

You might try showing one of two Monty Python interviews available on YouTube, like: "The Man with Three Buttocks". It's important that the interviewer and interviewee play it as straight as they can.

You can work out a format before you start. It might look like this:

The interviewer welcomes the audience, names the program, introduces him/herself and the guest, and tells us why the guest is of interest. Then the interview begins. The interviewer might prepare a list of questions beforehand.

*See page 32 for a list of possible interview topics.

Interview Topics:

The first person to cross the Pacific Ocean in a bathtub

A person training to eat a car

The person who teaches cats to play the piano

The person who is allergic to the word *because*

The person whose hair changes color according to their mood

The person who makes sounds for punctuation symbols when they speak (*Victor Borge*)

The person who is certain that they're a traffic light

The person who claps every time they think of something pink

The person who is afraid of swallowing their right hand

The person who's certain they smell of onions

The person who wants to update his brain

The person with a small live crocodile in their stomach

The person who bursts into tears when they hear someone yawning

The person who was abducted by aliens and returned convinced they're a rock star/xylophone/dinosaur/the ace of spades

The person who hears clouds talking to one another

The person who teaches trees to dance

The person who listens to mountains

The person who hears actual radio broadcasts in their head

You can add off-the-wall elements to interviews. For example, as the interview is going on three or four students are off in the background making animal sounds or noises with balloons. The interview people **_must stay on task and not laugh;_** or the interviewee might periodically make a strange sound or tie themselves in a knot around their chair as they speak or slap themselves as though being assaulted by mosquitoes; or the interviewer and interviewee might be sitting at a table which is at a slight slant; there's a ball on the table and one or the other of the two people keeps catching the ball as it rolls off the table and putting it back; or the interview has to be whispered for some reason, or sung; or one of the two people keeps getting cell phone calls about a strange situation like the person making the calls is trapped in a washing machine and can't get out and needs help, or is convinced that he/she is about to be attacked by a small group of Barbie's, and the person receiving the calls is trying to respond to these urgent messages and maintain an appearance of normality for the sake of the interview. If possible you might consider videotaping some or all of the interviews and watching them.

Lies

This activity develops students' ability to create scenarios, or stories, on the spot.

You say to a student – let's say it's Miranda – in tenth grade:

"Someone told me that you went missing when you were about 11 years old...your parents were very worried. Police were looking for you. Your picture was in the newspapers and on local TV and in shop windows. Your friends were sad. Then one day your mom heard a knock on the front door and when she opened it there you were. You told her that you had changed into a mermaid and had been living in the sea all that time. Is this true?"

Miranda thinks about this. If she says no you say okay and ask for a volunteer who's willing to try the mermaid scenario. If she says yes then you assume the role of the interviewer and question her about her experience.

"How come you turned into a mermaid? Where were you when it happened? Was it scary? Did you discover that your legs had turned into a long silver tail? Did you meet other mermaids? Any merguys?" and so on.

I remember one student who said that she was swimming in the sea and a big fish with rainbow-colored scales swam up to her and bit her gently on the forehead, and a kind of shiver went through her. Soon after that she felt herself changing. I remember another student with another lie – *"There's a rumor going round the school that you met Jesus one night"* – saying yes he did meet Jesus. He was walking home quite late one night and a man in the street caught up with him and started to talk to him and he realized very soon that this man was Jesus. This was one of the most moving and absorbing student scenarios I've ever heard.

Sometimes I've done "Lies" with two students at once, where the topic allows this. Sometimes I ask students to pretend to be operating TV cameras as the interview proceeds.

Sometimes a student will change the topic: *"No, that's not what happened. I didn't turn into a mermaid. I turned into Superman. I'd like to tell you about it."*

Possible Scenarios for "Lies":

Ability to levitate	Turned into a mermaid	Met Jesus
Abducted and returned by aliens	Turned into a centaur	Dragged away on a camping trip by a bear and raised as a bear cub for a year
Able for a week to read people's thoughts	Found a bag by the roadside with thousands of dollars in it	Saw an angel in a supermarket parking lot
Met the King (or Queen) of the Cockroaches	Went through a phase when your hair changed color according to your mood	Able to get people to say what you want them to say
Able to understand the language of birds	Able to breathe underwater	Run a dating service for ghosts
Able to tell when people are lying and when they're telling the truth	Keep a pet dragon in the garage/toolshed/deserted factory	Able to become invisible every Thursday evening

Question Dialogue

"We're going to play a game called question dialogue. What you do is have a conversation in which everything both people say is a question. You can talk about anything. The one guideline is that you don't get into routines like: Why do you ask why do I ask...Why do you ask why do I ask why do you ask...

Anyone willing to do question dialogue with me? Let's see if we can do five questions each."

This game calls for great speed of thought and creativity. A conversation might go something like this:

A. "Have you done your homework?"
B. "May I have a piece of chocolate?"
A. "Did you ever have that dream again?"
B. "The one about the purple lizards?"
A. "Who's going to put the garbage out?"
B. "Didn't I do it last week?"
A. "Did you answer my question about the dream?"
B. "Who ate all the chocolate?"

And so on. Once students have the hang of this game you can ask them to divide into twos and play it with one another.

Round Robin Stories

You can do this as a whole class or a small group activity.

"We're going to make up a story together. We'll agree on a title and then we'll take it in turns to add a sentence, one after another, and we'll see where it goes. You may be tempted, when it's your turn, to add a sentence that will make people laugh. This may not work in terms of the story, so try to resist the temptation.

Okay. Let's try it altogether to begin with just to see how it works. Anyone want to suggest a title? We'll think up three or four then vote for the one we prefer. "The face behind the mirror." Okay. Any others? "The fox with the blue tail." Good. Any more? "The deserted castle." Great titles. This is going to be a hard decision. Okay. Let's vote. Who wants to count the votes? Here we go. Number one... the face behind the mirror..."

Students are allowed to pass if they don't have an idea that fits the story. You can vote to stay with the one sentence unit or to extend it so that each student adds the equivalent of a paragraph. You can also introduce them to the idea of a separate story strand involving a separate character with the word: *meanwhile*. This makes things more complex, and may not work with younger students. But it gets very interesting when you have two story strands going on and you're looking for ways to bring them together for the conclusion. Sometimes the story that emerges is so good that a couple of students may decide to write it down and illustrated and turn it into a book, thus echoing the great historical movement from the oral to the printed culture.

(You might consider making cards of these story ideas and keeping them in a "Story Ideas Box" for students to dip into.)

Possible Story Titles:

The fox with the blue tail

The girl who couldn't smile

The silent bird

The ruined castle

The lost moustache

The Mother of the World

Hide-go-seek

How the snake made a friend

The flyaway helicopter

Box number seven

The third shoe

The invisible trousers

The path that changed its mind

Music of the stars

Footprints on the sand

The talking tattoo

Broken circle

The empty throne

The tree that learnt to dance

The lost unicorn

Big dogs and small children

The man on the roof

The unknown life of cell-phones

The old magician

The strange experience in the mall

The house of secrets

The blue island

The man who talks with dolphins

How Louise found true love

The sad hamburger

The shadow that dreamt of being solid

The skeleton that played the piano

The face in the window

Lights in the midnight sky

Story Starters:

When he woke up…

At first he thought he was alone…

He was having the flying dream again…

It looked like no one had been here for a long time…

When she opened the door…

She was hearing that sound again…

He found her in the kitchen talking to the broccoli…

He knew it was a mistake to smile at her…

Story Endings:

That was how he came to be walking backwards across the Golden Gate Bridge carrying a canary in a suitcase…

He smiled to himself and carefully slipped the fish back in the river…

After that Reuben Tomkins never lost an opportunity to talk to any horse he met…

From that day on she took no notice of anything the mirror told her…

Every time she sees a red bicycle she remembers that day…

So it was the wrong key after all but that didn't seem to matter any more…

Transformations

I pick up a pencil. I ask: "*What is it?* Left brain says '*It's a pencil.*' But right brain has other ideas. I sweep the pencil through my hair. "*It's a comb!*" I do a short series of mimes and the pencil becomes a flute, a toothbrush, a crutch, a telescope…I hand the pencil to a volunteer and it goes through more transformations. I produce a seashell, a pine-cone or a paper plate and each object undergoes transformations.

A more advanced stage of this activity is to be found in Viola Spolin's wonderful book Theater Games for the Classroom. It's called Transformation of Objects. If you google this title you'll find a description of the game.

These one-word responses are another opening of a door. Again we can look for ways to step into the room:

"Okay, you compared the pencil to a telescope. Who's holding the telescope? Where is he? What is he looking at? How far away is the thing he's looking at, or the person? What's he thinking as he gazes through the telescope? What's going to happen?"

This activity leads nicely into a writing exercise outlined later:

"Ways of looking"

<u>What Happens on Page 27?</u>

In my introduction to the left and right brain hemispheres I often talk about answers to left and right brain questions.

"A left brain question usually has only one right answer. How do you spell because? Who is the president of the United States? Right brain questions don't have a single correct answer. For example: What happens on page 27?"

I ask the question and pause. Silence. Students gaze at me blankly.

"There's no right answer. You make the answer up. You decide for yourself what happens on page 27. It's no good looking at me and telling me you don't know. Of course you don't know. There's nothing to **know**."

Finally someone says something like: "Joe dies." A minor wave of laughter may cross the room. But that's okay. Someone has responded. This is where it gets interesting, because what you're going to do is take this answer seriously and explore it. You ask questions. You work with the "Joe dies" student to uncover the details, to bring the answer to life. This process of asking questions, of working with the student to uncover details, is key to right brain work. "*Joe dies*" is the opening of a door. Your job is to persuade or help the student to step into the room and find out what's there. So the dialogue might go something like this:

"Where is Joe when he dies?"

"I don't know... on the beach."

"Is he by himself?"

"I think so."

"How old is Joe? Young, middle-aged or old?"

"Young."

"Is it morning, afternoon, evening or night?"

"Night. Late at night. "

"So here's this young guy Joe, on the beach late in the night by himself and he dies. Does he kill himself? Does he have a heart attack? Does someone kill him?"

"He doesn't die. He disappears."

At this point the student is taking charge of the story, which is what you're hoping for. You can feel the energy change. The other students want to know what's going to happen.

"Where does he go?"

"A boat arrives. Joe's been waiting for it. He sees a light flashing in the darkness. Then he sees the boat out beyond the waves where they break. It's waiting. He walks into the sea, throws himself forward and swims to the boat. Someone reaches down and helps him into the boat...."

We have crossed into the domain of the right brain. We are telling a story. We are imagining a place – the sounds, the look, the smells of a place. I remember the novelist Joan Didion speaking of an image that she saw in her head of a man landing in a parachute somewhere. She thought about this image. She asked herself questions about it, and a novel was born. The domain of the right brain is immense. It is full of memories and stories, images, conflicts and resolutions, deserts and mountains and valleys, strange beings, beginnings and endings. If you truly believe this when you work with students then they will follow you into right brain territory and make their own discoveries.

Initially, older students may find it harder to enter this domain. It involves taking risks, exposing yourself a little, and many adolescents are too self-conscious to do this easily. But there are always one or two who respond to the challenges you give them. Sometimes I introduce an idea – for example *What happens on page 27?* – and then ask the students to work in pairs or small groups, minimizing the exposure.

Because of this self-consciousness teenage students will often retreat into a defensive, shoulder-shrugging pose. A kind of "*whatever*" stance, with a hint of assumed boredom. You probably recognize this. It's understandable. But when the student drops this pose there's engagement, involvement, a flow of energy that everyone recognizes even if no one acknowledges it. When two or three students drop the pose one after another and engage themselves in the activity you've presented, they're enabling others to engage. The subtext is: *This is cool.* I sometimes comment on this. I mime the disengaged, "*This is, like, so boring...*" routine and point out – without making a big deal of it – that when we are totally involved in whatever's going on then we are living our lives to the full. If we hold ourselves back, do the shoulder-shrugging "whatever" posture then we're not. It's like driving a car with the brake on.

*See page 44 for a list of possible "right-brain" questions.

List of Possible Right Brain Questions:

What made the princess finally smile?

What does the golden door open to?

What did Michael say to the judge?

What did Andrew Filibuster do on the morning of September 15th, 2001?

What happened when he tried the invention out?

Who's tied up in the back of the car?

What did she find when she was digging in the back garden?

What did he have to do before he could cross the bridge?

Where and who was she when she woke up?

Yes/no Game

This is another game which develops the ability to think quickly and creatively. Person A asks questions. Person B answers them without saying yes or no on nodding or shaking their head or using sounds that mean yes or no like uh huh.

A. "Are you ready?"

B. "Yes."

A. "You're out."

A. "You want another chance?"

B. "Please."

A. "Is your name Jehosophat?"

B. "I wish it were... I think Jehosophat's a wonderful name."

A. "Is blue your favorite color?"

B. "It used to be, but now it's blue, isn't it?"

A. "Do you know what I'm going to say next?"

B. "Do you really want me to answer that question?"

SECTION THREE

Writing Warm-ups

Writing Warm-Ups

Adverb Repeats

A very simple structure that looks like this:

Dawn Scene

Silently silently

white mist floats over a white field

Softly softly

a pale sun rises over distant hills

Sweetly sweetly

birds are singing in wet trees

sweetly singing to the golden sun

- E.W.

Group Poems

Groups can be as small as 5 or 6, or as large as the whole class.(On the whole, the smaller the better.) Depending on the size of the groups, a number of sheets of paper are being circulated, each with a "power word" written on the top.

<u>Example:</u>

war music time hands mystery money shadow winter snake galaxy baby wolf ghost howl forest nightmare eagle school shock

Students add a line to what's already written on the paper when it reaches them. After a few minutes the writing is stopped, and the papers are read out loud.

Instant Poems

The emphasis here is on instant writing – with no concern about spelling or punctuation or whether what's written is any good.

I generally ask that lines be no longer than seven words (unless they need to be!) and that each line contains a verb. I pause between each line and watch the students. When it seems most of them are finished I give directions for the next line:

- Write a line containing the word river
- Write a line about a tree in winter
- Write a line 6 words long that includes a color
- Write a line you remember from a nursery rhyme
- Write a question in one line, and answer it in the next

Afterwards invite students to read through what they wrote. Give them some time to polish they want to. *You can take out lines that you don't like all that don't seem to fit. You can add lines. You can move them around. Read what you wrote about; sometimes your voice and it tell you what works and what doesn't.*

Here's another line by line challenge:

- Write a line about the sea
- Write a line about yourself that isn't true
- Write a line that includes a sound
- Write a line you remember from a song
- Write a line containing the words "here" and "there"
- Write another line about the sea

Knock-knock

When I explain what this exercise involves students invariably roll their eyes skeptically, but Knock-knock is a powerful demonstration of our ability to switch modes and create on the spot.

Students draw a line down the middle of a sheet of lined paper. (Or they can use 2 sheets of paper.) At the top of the left side they write a large A, and the title of a piece of descriptive writing:

The very tall man; The magic cave; The deserted school; The black horse; On the beach.

On the top of the right-hand side of the page they write a large B, and the title of a story:

The first date; The strange light in the sky; The face behind the mirror; The night of the great storm; The fox with the blue tail; The lost lion.

When the teacher knocks twice on a table or desk students start writing the descriptive piece. I usually side coach as they write:

"Keep your breathing deep and slow! Don't let the back of your tense your neck tense up – keep it loose; let your pen skim lightly across the page! Enjoy the flow of your ideas!"

Soon I knock twice again, and students switch to B, the narrative, and start writing *immediately.* Again I side coach, as above. I keep knock knocking. Students keep switching from one mode to the other. This goes on for five minutes or so.

Finally I call, "Finish the sentence you're on, then stop!

Okay...Breathe deeply, stretch...waggle your hands and fingers...

Now read through what you wrote...

Think about which mode you found easier...

If you want to continue with either of these please do.

SECTION FOUR

Writing Activities

Writing Activities

Bag of Words

Words for this activity are on page 180 at the back of the book.

Print them off, glue them to card and cut them up. It takes a while but it's well worth it.

This is a way into surreal writing.

"Here's a bag with a whole lot of words in it. I'm going to put a pile of words on your desks. Sort them out so that they're all facing up. I want you to arrange them so that they make lines, or phrases.

You can work in pairs.

Be grammatical – include subject verb object.

Get more words from the bag if you need them.

When you've made a line you like, write it down. Aim for at least four lines.

When you write your lines you can fill in any words you need that aren't in your pile."

Sample poems:

Music is Here
The rise of the sun
The fire of first romance
a forest burns
and music is here.
A murmur in a century
brings the light to disappear.
The sunset is a hole

in a mountain or valley.
The gallantful streaks of steam
and space mix together.

- E.W.

A New Island

The drums of the satin dragon
rise in the sun of April
a wish from words of a fire dance bird
splash in a glowing tide of sparkling fresh water springs.
The centuries return
and the opposite of anger is here.
We invite the brave knight to face a snake
to swim the waters
to disappear
and return.
You may come
but you may not return to your world.
With music, dancing and singing
you could drift in a picture
and summers are so warm and winters are just right.
You won't be gloomy on this island on a cloud
it's shocking but you can cross it
if you can make it
through the century.

- Aase Mitchell, 4th grade

Color Poems

"Let's have a look at colors as a subject for writing. Let's brainstorm all the color words we can think of. Close your eyes and visualize, without saying anything..."

Choose from the following list:

a bowl of cherries	a ripe strawberry	chocolate ice cream cone
flames in a fire	sunset over a calm sea	raindrops sliding down a window pane
autumn leaves	a big storm cloud	the smell and color of lavender
a rainbow	the color of your own eyes	the sky on a clear sunny day
a dandelion	the body of a wasp	a glass of orange juice

To avoid boring list poems – **Blue is the sunny sky/Blue is the color of my mom's eyes/Blue is a blue flower**...I ask students to think 'crazy', or 'sideways'. I talk a little about synesthesia, which is expressing sense impressions in terms of another sense (lots of information about this on the web.)

I ask them off-the-wall questions:

1. Is seven a hard or a soft number? What about three?
2. What color is the sound of a trumpet? Of a drum? A violin?
3. What is the sound of a hamburger's taste?
4. If someone is in a pink mood, how are they feeling?
5. What color is the name Catherine? (Or give them a choice: is Catherine a green name or a yellow name?)

6. Where does black go when it wants to hide?
7. Imagine a green sky. Imagine icy music.
8. What does Saturday taste like? Sound like?

Color poems can be written as though the color is talking about itself ("I" poem), as though the writer is talking to the color ("you" poem), or as a more detached description ("it" poem). Color poems lend themselves to visually rich displays.

Color Poem Prompts:			
Black	White	Red	Silver
Gold	Yellow	Blue	Green
Pink	Brown	Gray	Purple
Orange	Cream	Violet	Mauve
Turquoise	Vermillion	Beige	Khaki
Olive	Ivory	Magenta	Rose
Crimson	Lime	Teal	Navy
Dark	Light	Deep	Soft

Here's an "I" poem:

What Green Says to Me
Let me tell you
how I glow
where the long fern rises
in the dappled shadows
and the creek whispers and runs
and birds sing to the early morning.
I am soft
I am restful in my ways
I am there in the leaf cell and the grass blade
I am there, waiting under whiteness
when the cold snow falls
and is still
for I
am green.
- E.W.

Here's a "you" color poem:

Black
You are what I hear when nobody answers me.
You are the deep place at the back of the cave
Empty except for last night's dream.
You are all there was
before light was created
before snow on mountains
glowed white and pink
in the world's first morning.
- E.W.

(The "Let me tell you ..." beginning line is one that a lot of students have used.)

Color poems can be about two colors. This may lead to dramatic rather than descriptive writing:

Red and Yellow Get Married

I can burn, I am better!

Said Red.

I give people light, so I am better!

Said Yellow.

I am the one who makes the very valuable ruby red.

Said Red. So I am the best!

I am the one that gives long blonde silky hair. So ha!

Said Yellow.

I hurt when I squeeze out of your finger. So I win!

Said Red.

Will you marry me?

Said Red.

Will...you...marry...me...?

Said Yellow.

Sure.

Said Red.

5 years later...

Wow!   Our kids are orange!

Said Red.

No! Mom likes ME better...

- Arianna Carter-Monah, 3rd grade

Counting Poems

"We like lists. We like counting. Ten steps to a firmer stomach... 73 ways to save the world..."

This poem idea may seem too simple to be interesting, but it works. There are lots of things you can do with it because it's so simple.

Here's an example:

Green
One big hammer with a rusty head.
Two music boxes waiting to be would up.
Three big chunks of an unknown substance.
Four fierce animals at the foot of a tree waiting for you to climb down.
Five brothers asleep on a large coffin.
Six round white stones you remember seeing on the beach.
Seven stars too distant to be discovered.
Eight words in a fortune cookie.
Nine green socks with holes in them.
Ten candles burning on a birthday cake.
- E.W.

In "Green" the objects have nothing to do with one another.

Here's a very different application:

Domino Effect

Number 1 is playing dominoes with number 2
Number 2 is waiting for numbers 3 and 4 to come over for a
makeover
Number 3 is waiting for Number 4 to stop talking
Numbers 3 and 4 are waiting for number 5 to turn up with
the Chinese takeout
Number 5 is waiting for number 6 to give him some money
Number 6 is waiting for number 7 to give her the money she
owes him
Number 7 is waiting for her boss number 8 to give it to her
Number 8 is waiting for number 9 to get off the computer
Number 9 is waiting for a call from number 1 who's supposed
to be fixing her car
- E.W.

Possible Themes for Counting Poems:

Things I will do when I grow up

Things they found in the belly of the Great White Shark

Things the man in the coffee bar left behind

Things they found in her purse

Shapes I saw in the sky

What Crackernacks found on the beach after a big storm

What was found in the basement

The mad cheerleader's song

Creation Poems

Early in my teaching career, a long time ago in North London, I was required to teach Scripture to my class of 10 year-olds. I took the Genesis cycle of creation and made a big wall display of what was created the first day, the second day and so on. A cosmic schedule. I posted these lines by Dylan Thomas:

So it must have been after the birth of the simple light
In the first, spinning place, the spellbound horses walking warm
Out of the whinnying green stable
On to the fields of praise.

We created dance movements based on the cycle, using extracts from Stravinsky's The Rite of Spring:

How the first flower pushes from the buried seed, up through the soil,
rising towards the sky. How the first rabbit awoke and sniffed the air
and nibbled its first grass blade.

We followed this up with writing poems about creation. **The first raindrops. The first volcanic eruption. The first bird opening its beak for the first song.** The poems they wrote were wonderful. A sparkling stream of poems crossed my desk and entranced me. Later we took extracts from many of the poems, assembled them into a sequence, and used them as the soundtrack for a movie called The Creation of the World, using children's paintings, dances, poetry and music. We presented the whole thing to parents one evening in the school assembly hall.

This was my first experience of the innate creativity of children. It made a deep impression on me, and shaped my work as a teacher for the rest of my career. I think it worked so well because we had a strong, simple theme, we approached the theme from many angles, through a mix of forms, *and* our school principal was totally supportive.

'The Sun is a Golden Earring' is the title of a book published in 1962 and now hard to find. Natalia M. Belting, a folklorist, collected sayings which were the 'thoughts of men when they first looked in wonder at the heavens'.

Here are some examples:

Example #1

The Milky Way
is the sail of a great canoe
that floats among the stars
-Society Islands

Example #2

The moon is a white cat
That hunts
The grey mice of the night
- Hungary

Example #3

The Wind is a man with a spade in his hand.
He stands above the earth and shovels the winds.
He shovels the winds into the south
and the winds that blow into the north.
He shovels the winds to the east
and to the west.
-Lapland

Example #4

The winds dwell in the mountains
And when the Changeable wind blows
The animals wake from their winter sleep.
When the Blue wind blows, the leaves come out.
When the Yellow wind blows, the animals leave their dens
And the earth is covered with green growing things.
When the Dark wind blows, the snakes and the lizards
Shed their winter-dry skins and put on fresh skins.

-Navaho Indians

Example #5

When the gods are angry
they roll a stone across the floor of the heavens.
They roll a stone across the boards
that stretch from east to west across the skies.
They roll a stone across the boards
that stretch from north to south across the skies.
Men say it thunders.

-India

Example #6

The sun is a piece of rock crystal.
First Man fashioned it.
First Man chipped and smoothed and polished the crystal.
First Woman fastened white shells to the edge of it.
First Man made rays from sheet lightning and hung the sun in
the sky.
The sun is a piece of rock crystal.

- Navaho Indians

There are some simple techniques used in this series that are worth pointing out:

- Straightforward metaphor (1 and 2)
- Repeating first line at the end (6)
- Repetition: (3 and 4)

(The pattern in 4 can lead to powerfully rhythmic writing.)

Creation Poem Prompts:

Prompts to help get students started.

When the red rains fall…

When the blue clouds gather…

When the mountain trembles…

When the mountain hides its face…

When the sky is full of white birds…

When the sky is full of crimson fire…

When the eyes of the wolf are black…

"Imagine a small child asking a parent about how the stars came to be in the sky, or where the wind comes from, and the parent doesn't know the scientific answer but gives the child an image or a story drawn from the child's world that makes a kind of sense. I'd like you to choose one of the subjects from the list, or find one of your own, and write a small creation poem. Look again at the creation poems we read together and see how they're composed…often there's a list structure, like in the winds poems, or there may be a comparison, as in the Milky Way and the moon poems."

I suggest you have art materials available so that students can draw or paint before or after they write. There are more creation poems, and some children's paintings, on my website: www.emmanuelwilliams.com

The English poet Ted Hughes wrote some powerful creation poems.

Possible Subjects for Creation Poems:

Rainbow	Volcano	Mist	Snow
Ice	Frost	Earthquake	Fire
Flood	Rain	Sunset	Lightning
Thunder	Winter	Sun	Moon
Flowers	Hurricane	Night	Tides
Music	Wind	Mountains	Colors

Humans

Male	Female	Dreams	War
Love	Laughter	Music	Dance
Stories	Singing	Swimming	Painting
Jokes	Language	Babies	Teenagers

Creatures

Fish	Birds	Ant	Hawk
Dolphin	Dog	Cat	Tiger
Owl	Birdsong	Deer	Turtle
Bear	Otter	Snake	Pelican
Whale	Elephant	Mouse	Skunk
Slug	Butterfly	Spider	Bee
Chameleon	Lizard	Monkey	Panda

Plants

Rose	Reed	Lily	Ivy
Tree	Grass	Cactus	Holly
Sunflower	Redwood	Willow	Daffodil

Definitions

"The Meaning of Tingo" is a book of interesting words and phrases and their definitions collected from all over the world.

<u>Here are some examples:</u>

- **Nakhur** (Persian): a camel that won't give milk until her nostrils have been tickled
- **Areaodjarekput** (Inuit): to exchange wives for a few days only
- **Tsuji-giri** (Japanese): to try out a new Samurai sword on a passer-by
- **Marilopotes** (Ancient Greek): a gulper of coal-dust
- **Kapaau'u** (Hawaiian): to drive fish into the net by striking the water with a leafy branch
- **Neko neko** (Indonesian): someone who has a creative idea that only makes things worse
- **Serein** (French): rain falling from a cloudless sky

"Make up your own words – they can be strange rarely heard English words or words from another language, and give them definitions. You can work together, and come up with several words with definitions. If you're stuck here are some definitions you might like to make up words for" *(see next page for a list).*

Definitions:

Pick a definition and make up a word for it.

A very bushy moustache

Eating ice cream for the first time

The feeling a tree gets when it knows it's going to fall

Sniffing a roast potato without anyone noticing

The feeling you get when a ladybird lands on the back of your hand

A woman whose ears waggle when she talks

The frenzy that may come over a person in a shopping mall

The feeling a frog gets the first time it sees its reflection on the surface of a pond

Any big animal wearing a pirate's hat

A sneeze that's a lot bigger and louder than you thought it was going to

Words:

Pick a word and make up a definition for it.

Scumblehunk	Bongle	Mahaska	Boop
Pinkleshnitsky	Polly-wolly	Foggle	Goola-woola
Crunchcuckle	Lutter	Macshpliff	Daddle
Frag	Callibuster	Groon	Boll
Beezer	Noddlington	Neege-narge	Martify

Free Association

Write a "power word" on the board – a word with some resonance:

> secret...midnight...heart...birth...blue...storm...snake...
>
> tower...love...dream...heaven...tears...circle...sword...
>
> hair...witch...scream...hawk...hand...door...computer

Directions:

Choose a word, write it at the top of your page, then write whatever words come into your head for about 30 seconds. Don't worry about spellings. *thick tough strong hero*...

When the 30 seconds are up you can use your list as raw material for a poem, leaving out the words you don't need, changing their order, adding new words.

Here for example is a word association list starting with the word heart:

- heart
- beat
- drum
- pulse
- life
- death
- tomb
- stone
- bone
- marrow
- blood
- vein
- cut
- scar

And here's a very rough draft of a poem based on the list:

Deep drum thumps in my body

red blood dances

to the life beat

dances through vein and bone

dances under skin

under scars

flows behind eyes

makes strong the hero

as cold winds kiss the stony tomb

- E.W.

Free association writing can also be flowing phrases, rather than single words:

Heart

My heart is beating all the time thud thud thud...when I run it goes fast when I am sick it may go faster...I sometimes wonder what people mean when they say their heart is broken ...sometimes people draw the shape of a heart to mean love

- E.W.

Games

Young children make up games all the time. They share out the roles in their plays:

- "Pretend you're a robber"
- " 'tend I'm a...detective and Lizzie's an old lady..."
- " 'tend you're a princess and I'm a mermaid and this is my ship..."
- " 'tend you're a baddie and Lisa's a donkey and Emil's the man from the moon..."

After the casting the a story is sketched in:

"The old lady's in her rocking chair and she's just dropping off to sleep and the robber's creeping in through her back door..."

This is creativity in the raw.

I want you to think about the games kids play and the plays they make up. Think back to the games you used to play. Who made up the stories? Who was bossy? Who liked to win if it was a game? This makes an interesting subject for writing.

Here's a poem which takes a popular game further than it usually goes:

The Hide-go-Seek Game
Someone runs away and hides
Everyone else waits in the place called Home
Some are counting
Some are playing Pat-a-cake Julie
Some are watching the sky for clues.

The hider may pretend to be a tree or a starfish

or a wild boar or a broken down car
but this is dangerous and against the rules.
The tree might be cut down
the wild boar might be attacked by dogs
the starfish eaten by a lobster
the car towed away and crushed.

When all the numbers are counted
Everyone shouts "Coming ready or not!"
We leave the place called Home
and run off in different directions.

Some search the forest
Some climb behind the waterfall
Some crawl around in the bushes
Some check all the rooms in the house
all the cabins in the ship.
all the caves in the underground kingdom
Some examine the sea for footprints
The breeze for breathing
The river for reflections
Some look where rainbows begin
Somewhere thunder dies
Some climb the sky-high tree
at the end of the world
and gaze into the four corners of the cosmos.

The game is over
When the hider is found by the seekers
or when the hider reaches the place called Home without
being caught
or when it's time for dinner.
- E.W.

Places
Some be ins
Some be outs
Some be forwards
Some be backwards
Some be above
Some below
Some this side
Some that

Everyone has to look
for the middle

Some say it's in sky
But sky says I can't have a middle
Because I have no edge

Some say it's in circle
But circle says you can't come in

Some say it's here
But wherever here is
It says it's here
So then there has nowhere to go
And you can't have a here
Without a there

While all this is going on
A hole opens
And the middle slips away
And is lost forever
- E.W.

The "Games" theme also lends itself monologs and dialogues:

The Shop Game
This is my shop.
I'm selling handmade bumble bees
No I don't have any leprechauns for sale
Or dogs
No I don't have any money to sell you silly
You have to take them home and keep them warm
and then they start to bumble
and you take them outside and let them go and they
fly away to look for flowers.

If you're nice to them they come back.
Especially if you sing:
Come back little bumble
Come back to me
When you've finished with the flowers
In a couple of hours
Please come home for tea.

No these are special bumble bees that don't sting.
If they do sting you get your money back.
They like it if you breathe on them
and they like it if you give them a name.

I don't know if that one's a boy or a girl.

I think it depends on the time of the year.
Thank you and have a nice day.
- E.W.

Try writing your own game poem!

Game Poem Prompts:

The Faces and Mirrors Game	The Snakes and Ladders Game	The Sun Moon and Planets Game
The Bones and Stones Game	The Big Numbers and Small Numbers Game	The Hearts, Diamonds, Clubs and Spades Game
The Hole Game	The Fingers and Toes Game	The Dream Game
The Black and White Game	The Angels and Demons Game	The Truth and Dare Game
The Spiders and Flies Game	Journey and Road	Echo, Mouth and Ears
The Captain Midnight and the Shadows Game	The Cat and the Dog Game	The One with the Gun
The Brother Fire and the Sister Water Game	The "If I were the Richest Person In The World" Game	The Voice and Echo Game

I Would Paint a Picture

Writing a poem about a picture you'd like to paint is a smooth walk along the path into the imagination. It's basically a list poem, usually with no particular order, although there's often a change at the end. The picture can be light – as in Angel, or dark – as in War, or as in The Kiss, a tiny story. **Write a poem telling what would be in a painting you'd like to paint.**

The following are samples of poems for this activity:

Angel
I would like to wake up
and open my box of colors
and paint the small birds singing to the sky.
I would paint their songs
and the lines of their flying between trees.

I would paint an eagle
flying high above its shadow.

I would paint a blue butterfly
zig-zagging across a field of yellow flowers.

I would paint a quick wind
with coppery leaves in its hands
and a slow white snowfall
in a dark sky.

I would paint my dreams
and watch them come to life.

I would paint an angel
flying across the sky
leaving a trail of light blue music.

War

I would paint a picture of war
on a ripped scorched canvas
with bright reds and blood reds and smears of smoky black.
I would paint explosions and guns and shouting faces.
I would paint a man's hand clinging to a piece of wood from a
wrecked boat
or to a broken wall that was once part of his home
a hand at the end of an arm joined to the wounded body of a
human being
who refuses to die.
I would paint a picture of war
showing its horror and madness.

I would paint in the sky
beyond the fire and smoke and the stormy clouds
beyond the screaming and weeping and grieving
a faint gleam of golden light
so that there' d be something to hope for.

Kiss

I would paint a kiss
on a sheet of moonlight
with a brush made of shadows
and paint from a box of colors
never seen before
Some time after midnight
the kiss would drift
like a silvery smoke ring
in through your window
and hover over your sleeping face
and explode.

- E.W.

Imaginary Creatures

Our planet is home to a great range of fantastic creatures. Think of the duck-billed platypus. The hippopotamus. The giraffe. Even the dragonfly is extraordinary, when you think about it. Inspired by these creatures and by our creativity, we humans have created an enormous number of make-believe creatures.. Nearly every fantasy novel I've read features a fictitious creature of some kind. Making up creatures is something we do. The Loch Ness Monster. Bigfoot. The Centaur.

One way to write an imaginary creature poem is to write it as though the creature is speaking. So then the way it SOUNDS should be true to the creature. In my poem "Beast" there's repetition, which is like a slow drum beat.

Beast

My eyes are firestars
My hair is a prairie of black thistles
My mouth is the open gate at the end of the world
My breath is the source of the four winds
and the seven shades of purple
My voice is the whisper of cells and the explosion of rock
My hunger causes forests to hold their breath
My teeth are the gravestones of gods
My home is the space on the far side of time
My birth was the first big bang
My death will be the last
There is no name big enough for me

I once had a dream in which I was standing on a river-bank, and a large fish swam up to the surface just in front of me and stayed there, mouthing the current, waving its fins and tail. As I watched it a long slot opened along its back. Somehow I know what to do, and I took an envelope from my pocket and slipped it in the slot. The fish swam away to deliver it.

When I awoke I realized the phrase 'letter fish' had two meanings, and I started working on an ABC of Imaginary Fish. I'd choose a letter and wait. I imagined my mind was a clear stretch of water, and I'd wait for a fish to swim into it. Here's my "E" fish:

Elastic Fish
I'm a long one
And sometimes I'm a
looooooooooooooooooooooooooooooooooooooong
one
And sometimes I'm a
loooooooooooooooooooooooooooooooooooooooooooooooooooooo
ooooooooooooooooooooooooooooooooooooooooooooooooooooooo
ooooooooooooooooooooooong
one
Because the thing about me is I can make myself longer or shorter
whenever I want to.
I can stretch myself as long as I want. Well, nearly.
I can stretch all the way from England to France.
Last year my dad stretched all round the world.
An official elastic fish stretching record as a matter of fact.
We were so proud the day his tail knocked at the front door
while his head was out in the back garden eating sushi
and the rest of him was wrapped round the equator.
What happened then was
they were drilling for oil
somewhere off the coast of Indonesia
and they cut him in half
and his tail grew a head
and the police arrested mum for having two husbands.

Students like the mystery in Konga Fish. They often adopt the dialogue format it uses:

Konga Fish

What is your name?

Konga

Where do you live?

Down in the donkle deep

Who made you?

Fear made me

What shape are you?

I am the shape fear makes of me

Hog back bull horns

Fang of tiger

I am serpent

I am shark

I am Konga

What is the secret?

No!

What is the secret?

NO!

WHAT IS THE SECRET?

Where there is no fear

I disappear.

Directions

Think about the imaginary creature you want to create. It's often good to draw it first, color it, give it a name. Make the picture big so that it can be displayed later. As you draw it you can be thinking about these questions:

- What is its home?
- Does it have family?
- What does it eat/drink?
- How does it get its food and drink?
- What does its skin feel like?- Furry? Scaly? Hairy? Feathery? Smooth? Lumpy?
- How big is it?
- What sounds does it make?
- Does it have any friends?
- Does it have any enemies?
- What is its name?
- Does it have any special powers?

The poem doesn't have to answer all these questions. You can write as though the creature itself is speaking – "I", or as though you're speaking to the creature –"you" or about the creature –"it".

I've worked with students to put together a video entitled "Our Imaginary Creatures". If you want to try this, have the students do 2 or 3 pictures of their creature.

<u>For example:</u>

1. A young scumblehunk climbing a tree
2. Big scumblehunks fighting
3. A mother scumblehunk at home.

Having several pictures of each creature means you can pan the camera across the images as the student reads the poem. You can add variety by including shots of students as they work on their creatures and as they read their poems. If you can add background music – preferably composed and played by the students - so much the better.

Possible names for Imaginary Creatures:

Scumblehunk	Razzer	Ponkle	Blackhair
Slinkyslider	Moonsnake	Skinnytube	Loobadooba
Skrank	Boxhead	Finky Winky	Skyfox
Shadow Wolf	Wulloper	Icicleteeth	Champelorum
Mudhead	Wobbleguts	Slimebones	Popsidoodle
Firemouth	Tweetlepops	Razor-fangs	Stoneface

"Imaginary People" is a good spinoff from this theme:

Cracklebones
crackle crackle crackle
you can hear him coming
his bones crackle and snap
like the sound of dead twigs when you step on them
like crisps when you open the bag.

Every time he moves
crackle crackle crackle
when he folds his arms
when he cleans his teeth
when he bends to do up his shoe laces
when he goes upstairs or down
when he walks along the street
when he swims in the public pool
when he rides his bike
when he stirs his tea
when he eats an apple
when he plays the guitar
crackle crackle crackle
When he gets into bed

his wife puts cotton wool in her ears
When he shifts and crackles in his sleep
she dreams of forest fires
tons of rice crispies popping in a sea of milk
matchstick mice doing gymnastics
and millions of icicles
creaking and crackling in sudden gusts.

He used to get depressed about having crackly bones
until he joined an organisation of people whose bodies do
strange things
like the baby girl in Australia
who grows ten and a half inches every full moon
and an old lady in Brazil with a live canary in her right lung
and a Norwegian sailor whose skin is totally transparent.

They all meet once a year.
Cracklebones wants them to do a TV show.
He thinks they can make a lot of money.
- E.W.

Possible names for "Imaginary People" poems:

Barbed-wire Man	Bubblemouth	Jelly Baby
Mrs. Misty	Leapy Lou	Rainbow Princess
Gigglebox	Needlenose	The King(or Queen) of Concrete
Loonygan	Sassparassparasp	Rubber Robby

Journey Poems

"A hero ventures forth from the world of common day into a region of supernatural wonder: fabulous forces are there encountered and a decisive victory is won: the hero comes back from this mysterious adventure with the power to bestow boons on his fellow man."

- Joseph Campbell

There are thousands of stories about journeys. They're often about someone who leaves home, has a series of adventures and goes through some kind of change, and returns home. So it's a circle, or, more accurately a spiral, since the person who went on the journey isn't the same when he or she returns home. Think The Hobbit, or Alice in Wonderland, or Narnia.

Here's a very simple journey poem:

Snake's Journey

Snake went on a journey.

Snake came to a wall.

Snake climbed the wall.

On the other side of the wall was a pool.
He swam across the pool and came to a river.
He swam across the river
And came to a cave.

He went into the cave and slept.

While he slept

Snake dreamt he was a bird.

The bird went on a journey.

He flew into a cloud.

In the cloud was a forest.

The bird flew into the forest.

In the forest was a fire

The bird flew into the fire.

The fire burnt him up

Leaving the bones.

The bones said, "We are snake".

They joined together

And snake came out of the ashes.

Snake looked around.

He saw he was in a cave.

He came out of the cave.

He swam across the river.

He swam across the pool.

He climbed over the wall

And went home.

It's a story poem. Short lines. Very simple language. No adjectives. One thing happens, then the next thing. One place then the next. Quite a lot of repetition.

"Why do you think the snake dreamt that he was a bird?"

(Give students time to think about this and come up with some responses)

Perhaps it's because snake always lived close to the ground that he dreamt of flight, of being **up there** instead of **down here**. When he came back to being snake he still had the memory of flying within him, so he was more than he was before the journey.

Choose your creature. Find one that's special to you in some way. Think about the journey your creature takes, about the change that happens to your creature. You can draw a map of the journey first.

The transformation in the journey can be brought about by a dream, or a ritual, or a spell, or a powerful natural event like a huge storm (Wizard of Oz), or being swallowed by a very large creature (Jonah), or going into a long sleep and then waking up. It can come about as the result of crossing some kind of threshold or portal, like the Narnia children going through the back of the wardrobe, or Alice falling down the rabbit hole. It can come about after meeting someone with power, like Gandalf, or after a near-death experience.

*See the following page for a list of possible creatures and another list of places.

Creatures:

Serpent	Dragon	Cat	Shark
Dolphin	Worm	Wolf	Bee
Fox	Bear	Deer	Coyote
Lizard	Salamander	Phoenix	Scorpion
Salmon	Whale	Rabbit	Toroise
Bull	Bird	Monkey	Dog
Firebird	Spider	Frog	Hawk
Toad	Pig	Ant	Horse

Place:

Cave	Abyss	Pit	Tunnel
Mountain	Ocean	Waterfall	Highway
Desert	Night	Fog	Storm
Clouds	Volcano	Swamp	Flood
Fire	Forest	Rainbow	Iceberg
Tower	Castle	Door	Corridor
Trap	Boat	City	Dungeon
Wall	Labyrinth	Tower	Burrow

Transformations:

Falling down a hole or well	Gift	Death/resurrection	Dream
Mirror/reflection	Spell	Music	Shedding skin

Here's a student's journey poem:

Bird's Journey
I am the bird
Who flies in deep skies
And has feathers of gold, blue and red.
As I fly I behold in wonder
The stars and the sun
I flew down to the earth
And slept on top of a tree
And in my dreams were fires
And lying dead was me
I woke and was not tired
I felt different in the same way
I looked in the rivers
And saw a panther dressed in black
With fiercer eyes than any
That danced spitting flames.
Protector and majestic hunter
Was the spirit I'd become.
I prowled throughout the day
And hunted in the night
My spirit will not be tamed
For my dream has taken flight.
-   Gabriella Cruz

Looking Inside Me

We tend to think of ourselves as one person, and in a way that's true…but it's also true to say that we're different people, all with the same name, all living inside our skin. I like distant beaches, for example, where I can walk and sing and write and look at the sea and be totally alone…but I also love being with my friends, talking and laughing around a dinner table. This poetry idea is about looking inside ourselves and identifying the different characters – not necessarily human – inside us, and writing about them.

You might use the guided tour (see below); a walk round a gallery or exhibition of photos or paintings; a circus with a circus master; the crew of a ship or a space craft; the cast of a movie starring and all about you; the inhabitants of an island; or the members of a large household (each member having different skills and responsibilities).

You could draw portraits of each of the characters inside you. Even give them names, or nicknames.

Here's an example of the tour idea:

Guided Tour
Good afternoon ladies and gentlemen
Welcome to my Home Exhibition
Let me show you around.
Please stay with the group
things could get dangerous.

Here's the library
curtains closed as usual
this is the scholar sitting with his books

Here's the tower
where the dreamer sits by the window
watching the clouds and the edge of the forest
waiting for something to happen

This is the nursery
here the little boy plays with his toys
this is where the good guys always win

Big dude in the gym
lifting weights
tough dude
look in his eye says Keep outta my way.

There's another door
down that corridor
We won't be going in there
Not today
- E.W.

A friend wrote a rich choral speech piece based on this idea. Here's an extract:

Actor
There is a frog in me
A queen-like small one
A royal amphibian who hops about with joy
And the pasture of green animals
Will not let it go
Actor
There's always been a whistle in me
A fluty object that turns on my access to music
Whether it be from silent movement
Or from the bright vocal machine

And the saint of music
Will not let it go

Actor
There is a cat in me
A fragile living creature asking for attention
But in a silent and barely noticeable way
Wanting to be fed with
True and loving desperate comfort
And the soul to create love will not let it go

Actor
There's a rubber band in me
It gets pulled a long way
All day, until it can no longer stretch nor
Keep its wide strength spread
But go "pop"
And be motionless
Until it is ready to stretch again
And the bright power of work will not let it go

Actor
There is a bouncy ball of anger in me
It bounces with uncontrollable speed
Jumping up and down
Having no way of stopping
Until it's been caught in the hand
And touched softly
And be helped to lessen its temper
And the rubber hot heat of passion will not let it go

Claudia
Oh I've got animal and vegetable and mineral in me
An invisible landscape of love and fear and imagination

A menagerie of creatures prowling the jungle
A mountain of steel
A garden of flowers, blossoming in spring and fading in autumn
And the angel of joyful life will not let it go.

- Claudia Bocock

Metaphor Game

"Poetry provides the one permissible way of saying one thing and meaning another...Unless you are at home in the metaphor, unless you have had your proper poetical education in the metaphor, you are not safe anywhere."
- Robert Frost

Metaphor Game takes us deep into right brain country. The idea is to write a poem about someone you know using a selection of the following:

Metaphor Game Word Selection:

Music	Furniture	Place in nature
Color	Taste	Weather
Movie	Painting	Musical instrument
Animal	Story	Season
Food	Sport	Car
Country	Island	Garden
Part of the body	Piece of equipment	Item of furniture
Building	Video game	Shape

I often begin with something like the following:

> "So, you know me a bit as a person...if I were a piece of music, what kind of music would I be?"
> "Classical," says someone.
> "Okay. Classical. Fast, medium pace, or slow?"
> "Fast."
> "Solo instrument or group...big orchestra? "

94

"Orchestra"

"Where's it playing, this orchestra? Remember, this is poetry. Anything's possible. The orchestra could be playing on a remote beach, or a mountain top, or in an empty gym..."

"In a school playground."

"Great! Anyone listening?"

"Bunch of kids."

"Okay...so here's the beginning: 'He's a fast piece of music played by a symphony orchestra to a bunch of kids in a playground.' Is that it?"

"Yeah."

"Okay. If I were an animal what animal would I be?"

"Eagle."

"Great. Can you describe this eagle?"

And maybe we end up with:

"He's an eagle soaring high above the clouds waiting to swoop down on poems."

By this time they're usually ready to write their own Metaphor Game poems.

"You don't have to use all the ideas in this list. Don't start your lines with 'If he was a animal he would be...' – go straight into it. Write about someone you know well, like a family member, or a friend. Or you can write about yourself. If you write about yourself I suggest you make it a 'he' or 'she' poem. This may give you more freedom. And remember...everyone has light AND dark aspects to their nature. Look for metaphors that show this. "

One of my favorite Metaphor Game lines was written by a 7th grader about a friend:

"He's a tropical island waiting to be discovered by girls."

Before running a Metaphor Game workshop try writing one yourself so that you're familiar with it. I usually post the ideas up and talk about them a little, read one or two Metaphor Game poems, then work with the students on a group Metaphor Game poem, as shown above.

Here's one – pardon my vanity! – a seventh grader wrote about me:

Emmanuel
He's a Dumbledore, wise and magical
He's a triple-decker sandwich you never stop enjoying
He is flowing classical music with rock and roll explosions
He is a mural, pastel but vibrant, with a little of everything
He is a flamboyant peacock showing his colors
He is a sophisticated Italian sports car zipping through the streets of London
He is a comfortable rocker in a gazebo that makes you want to stop and think
He is a quill pen with never-ending ink, so you can write forever.

Here's one by a sophomore:

He's my pain
He's a hardcore metal song, playing the guitar solo in his mind
He's a coffee table only used for coffee
He's the cut I hate to remember
He's a bitter taste that dries up in my mouth
He's the rain cloud that just won't go away
He's the movie that disappoints you
He's a sharp dull red that burns my eyes
He's an annoying voice in the back of my head
He's the situation you can't get out of
He's the person I love to hate
- Sarah Eisenbarth

Usually there are two or three students who can't get going. What to do?

"Can't think of anything? Okay. May I borrow your pen? Thanks. I'm going to ask you questions and write the answers so you can be free to think. Now... who's your poem going to be about?"

"I don't know."

"Sister... brother? "

"My mom."

"Okay. So. You know your mom, you know what she's like. If your mom were a color, would she be a bright color or more of a quiet color?"

"Bright."

"Yellow? Red? Orange?"

"Yellow."

"Like a sunflower?"

"Like the grass on the hills in the summer."

"Nice! She's the yellow of the grass on the hills...now, do you want to say on the hills in the summer or on the summer hills?"

"...on the summer hills."

"She's the yellow of the grass on the summer hills...You like that?"

"Yeah."

"Now, if your mom was an animal would she be a big animal, medium sized or small?"

"Big."

"Wild or..."

"She's a big lively dog..."

"What color is this dog?"

"If I go away now can you keep going? The list's up there on the whiteboard. Okay?"

"Yeah." And the student takes back the pen.

My World

If you can, take your students outside for this exercise so that the world can enter them through their senses and bring them ideas. If not, make available lots of nature pictures, preferably mounted on card and laminated.

"Poetry can take us places we don't normally go. In 'My world' you're going to imagine what it's like to be a creature or a plant or even something like a creek or a stone, and write as though this creature or plant or whatever is telling you about its world."

<u>Example:</u>

Shoal
I move you move
it moves all around us
and we move through it
and it moves us

you and I are one
and you and you and you and you
and all of you are one
we are one
we move as one
and it moves all of us as one

and all the smells of it and sounds and tastes
dips and liftings and the long strong flowings
from before behind us
all of this we move through
and the silverings of waterlight
the quick sucked breaths
and the shockwave jolt of fear we move through

scream the single scream from each gaped mouth
the sudden horrorhole
that sucks us down

haze of whisperings the criss-cross trails
rippling before behind among
hoverings the sudden dartings
through the sparkle and the dark of it
and all the smells of it and sounds
and dips and liftings of it
and the long strong flowing from behind before
all this we move and move through
all of us are moved
by what we move through.
- E.W.

Here's a student poem on this theme:

A Baby Whale in its Mother's Belly
I live in darkness
Gently swaying in a warm bubble
My body is small but it is growing
With each day I feel more cramped
As I lie in my dark bubble
Gently, gently I feel the warm water
Being sucked away.

I feel my fin an a small opening
I too am sucked into a strange world
Light touches my small eyes
New but cold water surrounds me

I'm pushed into the air
As I breathe my first breath.

'My World" poems don't have to be about creatures.

The Wind

Don't ask me where I'm going
says the wind
Don't ask me to stop and think.
I've got too much to do
shoving clouds across the sky
bending trees and stirring lakes and seas.
I scatter seeds and leaves and rain.
I fling myself at birds and hilltops.
I shake things up
stir things around
separate what's dead from what's alive.
I race through space
like waves of mad loud music.
You will see treetops dance until they're dizzy
white flakes whirl until they're giddy.
You will see the air blown clear of smoke and dust
the blue sky stripped to deeper blue
starlight flash like frost.
My name is Cloud-shover
My name is Grass-rippler
My name is Bough-breaker
My name is Sea-stirrer
King Roar of the roaring woods.
I am wild and strong and free.
I am the force you feel
but never see.

- E.W.

Possible subjects for "My World" Poems:

What would the world be like according to a...

Chicken in a battery farm	Ant in an anthill
Sea anemone, or crab, in a tidepool	Baby whale inside its mother's belly
Tiger in a zoo	Canary in a cage
Circus elephant	Deep sea fish
Tapeworm	Honey bee
Aquarium fish	Jellyfish
Mole in a burrow	Baby bird inside an egg, or a nest
Pig in a sty	Puppy in a pound
Bee in a hive	Worm in soil
Spider building a web	Eagle high in the sky
Salmon leaping up a waterfall	Mole digging a tunnel
Bat catching flying insects	Dolphin leaping across wavetops
Horse galloping across a field	Monkey swinging through trees

Or, extend the "My world" idea to include other realms:

Snowflake	Snowman	Cloud
Autum leaf	The wind	Rose
Old, tall tree	Moss on a wall	Grain of beach sand
Ocean wave	Feather	Bone
Spider web	Ripe cherry	Earthquake
Raindrop	Forest fire	Old empty house
Dollar bill	School desk	Skateboard

"Not" Poems

"Everything is what it is because it's not something else. A school desk is a school desk because it isn't anything else...it's not a saucepan of hot milk or a lizard or an earthquake or a dog's tail. Also, if you're listening to this it's because you're not sitting in a boat fifteen miles out to sea fishing for salmon, or playing lead guitar in a big amphitheater concert, or dying in the American Civil War. All this is obvious, in a way. So obvious we don't usually stop to think about it. Of course you're not a stapler. Neither are you a young wolf, nor are you a cabbage."

Not poems are basically lists. Here is an example:

Not a Strawberry
Here is
our
gingercat
See how lightly he leaps
up on to the couch beside me
Hear him purring like a muffled engine as he
snuggles up against my arm
And I think it only fair to tell him that
he is not a peacock
with a tail like a vision of beauty at the end of the world
and a screech of a shriek oh no and he's not
an empty tennis court or an obsolete bulldozer
or a dragon or an old tree in the rain
and his name is not Peppervich
and neither is it Siegfred and furthermore it is not
Jonathan and he's not going to explode any time soon
or turn green or climb to the top of the Big Rock Candy
Mountain
because his name is Mishka
and he is our gingercat
oh yes
- E.W.

Here's a Not poem by a high school student:

The Not Poem

An electric guitar is a musical instrument.

It is used to play out the soul and express for the heart,

Or is can wake your parents, resulting in an allowance reduction.

It is not a fancy car used to impress girls at school,

Nor is it a slab of cake that will make one fat,

And it will never be the obese cat launching itself onto the couch.

It is not a pair of scissors snipping away strands of matted hair,

And it is not a gleaming sword plunged into a dragon's heart.

It is not a midget waddling through the halls during class times,

Thus it is not a cardboard box rotting in the basement.

It is not a beautiful fragment of gemstone of which collectors seek,

And it is not a pair of glasses used to make the billboard clearer.

As such, it is not a communist nation seeking to destroy capitalism,

An electric guitar is simply an electric guitar.

- Justin Kwok

Warm-ups for Not poems

Let's do some quick don't stop to think about it, oral warm-ups.
Ready?

- Name five things that are yellow!

- Name five things that are **not** yellow and you can't just name other colors.

- Tell me six things you can't do with a wet diaper.

- Five things that are not a hammer.

- Six things that are not in your backpack.

- Several things you can't do with a piece of cheese.

- Several words that do not start with A.

Not Poem Prompters:

Try writing a Not poem

Seven things that are not a rabbit	A list of things that are not what you might have for breakfast
A number of things a chimpanzee would not do	Things you wouldn't say to a frog
Things that are neither a cup nor a saucer	Several places where you won't find bananas

---

Pattern/structure Poems

Pattern is very important in music, dance, design and poetry as well as the natural world. Many of the first poems kids hear – the Mother Goose nursery rhymes – are little more than patterns made with rhyme and repetition:

Doctor Foster went to Gloucester
In a shower of rain.
He stepped in a puddle
Right up to his middle,
And never went there again.

Oh the grand old Duke of York
He had ten thousand men
He marched them up to the top of the hill
And he marched them down again.
And when they were up they were up
And when they were down they were down
And when they were only halfway up
They were neither up nor down.

The great thing about these pattern poems is that they provide a simple, clear structure for your ideas. They have a list dynamic. Here are 4 examples of pattern in poetry, each done in a different way.

The first one's very basic:

1. Repetition

The repeated, or parallel, structure is a great way to write a poem that *sounds* like a poem. Here's one by a 4th-grade UK student:

The Wind Speaks

I am the wind
I whisper to the whirling world
I am the wind
I whisper to the waves, the wonderful waves
I am the wind
I am the whispering wonderful wind.
I have a secret
the secret that blows the breeze away
to an unknown land
I have a secret
that topples the tall trees
like a terrible tornado.
I have a secret
that nobody knows.
– Ian Smith

Sometimes I project this poem, then read it aloud, have a couple of students read it as a choral speech piece, with one reading the repeated lines and the other the longer lines, then ask students to tell me anything they notice about the poem. (You can organize this as a small group discussion if this works better for you.) It's important I think to hold back on the points you want to make about the poem – use of repetition, difference between the verses, the sound of the poem (assonance), and give kids the space to make these discoveries for themselves. The more we can do this, the more confident students are with the ways poetry works.

Here's another repeated structure poem. This one is based on a cumulative pattern, like "I have a basket." This structure works with 1st and 2nd graders.

Fly
fly is small
fly is small and quick
fly is small and quick and buzzy
fly is small and quick and buzzy and busy
fly is small and quick and buzzy and busy and black
fly is light as a petal
fly is quick as a breeze
you'll never catch fly
'cos fly can fly.
- E.W.

Here are two very different repetition poems that I wrote.

This poem has a magical, incantatory ring:

Winds
The winds dwell in the mountains,
and when the changeable wind blows
the animals wake from their winter sleep.
When the blue wind blows
the leaves come out
When the yellow wind blows
the animals leave their dens
and the earth is covered with green growing things
When the dark wind blows
the snakes and the lizards
shed their winter-dry skins
and put on fresh skins

The second is based on my memories of telling my kid sister – with an air of authority – outrageous lies. This is a theme – and form – that lots of students have taken to:

<u>Carrots</u>

My brother said
carrots are rude.
My brother said
if I get soap in my bellybutton my bum will fall off.
My brother said
carrots can see in the dark
and if you eat too many you turn into an owl.
My brother said
the world's hollow, like an Easter egg
and if I play jump rope on the back lawn
I'll break it open and fall in and be lost forever.
My brother said
people go bald because their brain eats their hair.
My brother said
icicles are the ghosts of dead carrots
My brother said
breaking a spider's web
eating frogspawn
seeing a tooth fairy
stroking cats the wrong way
putting your shoes on the wrong feet
losing stones with holes in them
forgetting to hold your breath in tunnels
yawning and sneezing at the same time
are all bad luck.
My brother's silly
I never eat frogspawn.

<u>Possible themes for a poem similar to the above:</u>
- When the rains gather in the sky
- When the mountain trembles
- When the air holds its breath
- When the birds fly into clouds

2. "Simile Dance"

Let's have a look at an example for "Simile Dance". As you'll see there's lots of repetition. Nothing makes any sense in this poem. Notice how the last verse echoes the first. This "circle" structure is a useful one to remember. Four strong beats in each line; AA BB CC DD rhyme scheme.

> There was a man with one blue eye
> Who made his wife an apple pie
> And when the pie began to bake
> 'Twas like an island in a lake
>
> And when the lake began to freeze
> 'Twas like a shipwreck on the seas
> And when the seas turned into fog
> 'Twas like a giant lost his dog
>
> And when the dog began to beg
> 'Twas like a mountain laid an egg
> And when the egg began to crack
> 'Twas like a pig inside a sack
>
> And when the sack begins to fly
> You'll find the man with one blue eye
> And if his wife is double nice
> She'll serve you up a double slice.

> **Here's a list of possible first lines for "Simile Dance":**
>
> | | |
> |---|---|
> | There was a man with twenty toes | There was a girl who stole the wind |
> | There was a king who lost his throne | There was a boy who learnt to fly |
> | There was a man who drank the sea | There was a dog that couldn't bark |
> | There was a bird lived on the moon | There was a house that ran away |
> | There was a ladder reached the sky | There was a tree that learnt to dance |

3. "Meet-on-the-Road"

"Meet-on-the-road" is a dialogue poem that tells a story. Here is an example:

> "Now, pray, where are you going, child?"
> said Meet-on-the -Road
> "To school sir, to school," said Child-as- it- Stood.
> "What have you in your basket, child?"
> said Meet-on the Road
> "My dinner sir, my dinner,"
> said Child-as- it- Stood.
> "What have you for your dinner, child?"
> said Meet-on-the -Road
> "Some pudding, sir, some pudding," said Child-as- it- Stood.
> "Oh then I pray, give me a share," said Meet-on-the -Road
> "I've little enough for myself, sir," said Child-as- it- Stood.
> "What have you got that cloak on for?"
> said Meet-on-the -Road

"To keep the wind and cold from me," said Child-as- it-Stood.
"May the cold wind blow through you,"
said Meet-on-the -Road.
"Oh what a wish! Oh what a wish!" said Child-as- it- Stood.
"Pray, what are those bells ringing for?"
said Meet-on-the -Road.
"To ring bad spirits home again," said Child-as- it- Stood.
"Oh then I must be going child," said Meet-on-the -Road.
"So fare you well, so fare you well," said Child-as-it-Stood.

-    E.W.

Here's a list of possible characters:

You'll need two of these to have a dialogue, but you can always include more.

Beast-in-the-cage	Boy-as-he-went	Old-woman-who-laughed
Bird-in-the-Tree	Man-in-the-Moon	Thief-in-the-Night
Voice-in-the-Wind	Wolf-at-the-Door	Babe-in-the-Womb
Star-as-it-Shone	Song-as-it-sang	Feet-as-they-danced
Bone-in-the-Grave	Meet-in-the-Forest	Bullet-in-the-Gun
Ghost-in-the-Shadows	Cat-at-the-Window	Love-that-is-lost
Soldier-who-marches	Mother-who-brings-peace	Clown-who-weeps

4. "The Door"

No need to analyse what's going on in this poem. It's a
list. Notice the echo of the first line in the last.

Try reading with 2 people reading alternate lines.

The Door

A child knocked at the door and it opened on to a playground.

A policeman knocked on the door and it opened on to a
prison.

A poet knocked on the door and it opened on to a forest.

A hermit knocked on the door and it opened on to a party.

A saint knocked on the door.

The door turned into light.

A blind man knocked on the door and it opened on to a dark room
full of birdsong.

A traveler knocked on the door and it opened on to a distant
horizon.

A Christian knocked on the door and it opened on to a
mosque.

A soldier knocked on the door.

It opened when he lay down his gun.

He stepped inside and found himself at home.

A suicide bomber knocked on the door and it opened into a room
full of her victims, and the children of her victims and the children
her victims would have had if they hadn't been killed.

A politician knocked on the door and it opened into a room
full of politicians knocking on doors.

A homeless man knocked on the door and it opened a little
way then closed again.

An extra-terrestrial knocked on the door and it flew away

A carpenter came and made another door.

A child knocked at the door.

- E.W.

Character Ideas for "The Door":

You might want to list your characters before you start the poem.

King	Beggar	Dancer
Ghost	Poet	Madman
Banker	Millionaire	Farmer
Pirate	Soldier	Baby
Eagle	Queen	Alien
Builder	Criminal	Judge
Cop	Healer	Magician
Athlete	Singer	Journalist
Priest	Hunter	Orphan
Geek	Angel	Hunter
Snake	Butcher	Artist
Mermaid	Robot	Knight
Twins	Comedian	Puppy
Explorer	Chef	Hero

Alternatives for "The Door":

Obviously "knocked" won't work for for most of these. If you like you can use The Door but change the characters.

The Window	The Sky	The Fire
The Room	The Hole	The Sea
The Future	The Chest	The Painting
The Cave	The Key	The Mountain
The Heart	The Gate	The Wall
The Room	The Palace	The Bridge

5. Limericks

(Full disclosure – I have a book of limericks on Amazon called "There was an Old Lady from Bristol)

This is a tricky form. Best for older students. The rhyme scheme's AA BB A. The structure is two longer lines, two shorter lines and a longer line which is the same length as lines 1 and 2. The rhythm is best tapped out rather than analyzed. The first line introduces the character; line 2 begins the story; lines 3 and four continue the story; line 5 is the ending.

I've included some sample limericks followed by a series of first lines.

Sample limericks:

> **There once was a shepherd named Miller**
> **Whose favorite film was Godzilla.**
> **He fed all his sheep**
> **On chunks of raw meat**
> **Now they leap through the trees like gorillas**

> **There once was a fellow named Crane**
> **Who decided to eat a small train.**
> **He began with the engine**
> **But got indigestion**
> **So he ate an old tractor in Spain.**

> **There's a father I know named Crenshaw**
> **Who likes to pretend he's a seesaw.**
> **Took his kids to the sea**
> **And someone told me**
> **She saw a seesaw on the seashore.**

Example first lines for Limericks:

There once was a quarrelsome wizard

The house that was lonely and cold

The lady whose name was Christina

There once was a parrot named Vicky

The old man who lived in a cello

Said the man with a hole in his hat

Said the girl who was born in a tree

There once was a Wozard of Iz

There once was a fellow from Bath

The servant who wished to be king

There once was a dentist named Tooth

There was a young fellow named Tom

There was an old lady from Gotham

There once was a lady named Ruth

There once was a fairy named Maggy

There once was a waterfall queen

There once was a fellow named Mark

There once was a grumpy old pig

People Descriptions

"People Descriptions" is another surreal writing idea. It's a deliberately over-the-top, exaggerated description of a person using wild images, and based on the list structure.

<u>This is an extract from Andre Breton's poem Free Union:</u>

My wife whose thoughts are summer lightning
Whose waist is an hourglass
Whose waist is the waist of an otter caught in the teeth of a tiger
Whose mouth is a bright cockade with the fragrance of a star of the first magnitude
Whose teeth leave prints like the tracks of white mice over snow
Whose tongue is made out of amber and polished glass
Whose tongue is a stabbed wafer
The tongue of a doll with eyes that open and shut
Whose tongue is incredible stone
My wife whose eyelashes are strokes in the handwriting of a child
Whose eyebrows are nests of swallows
My wife whose temples are the slate of greenhouse roofs
With steam on the windows
My wife whose shoulders are champagne
Are fountains that curl from the heads of dolphins under the ice
My wife whose wrists are matches
Whose fingers are raffles holding the ace of hearts
Whose fingers are fresh-cut hay
My wife with the armpits of martens and beech fruit
And Midsummer Night
That are hedges of privet and nesting places for sea snails

Whose arms are sea foam and a landlocked sea
My wife with eyes that are forests that are forever under the
axe
My wife with eyes that are the equal of water and air and
earth and fire
- Andre Breton

Here's one of mine:

Girl with a Watering Can
A painting by Renoir
her hair is the breath of a salamander dreaming in the sun
the ribbon in her hair awakens the cockerel
it is the first flame dancing in the sky
it is the big bang awaiting an echo
her face is a sweet little cuddlebun
even when closed her mouth speaks of important questions
her dress is a bell echoing the sea's deep places
embossed by a haberdashery of stars
her boots are where they should be
if they are to fulfill their destiny
in her right hand she holds history
in her left hand she holds a gift for maman.

Obviously you're not trying to write an accurate description.
You're going wild with words.

List of people to write over-the-top descriptions of:

The Very Tall Person	My Brother	My Sister
The Weight-lifter	The Warrior	The Rock Musician
The Geek	The Cheerleader	The Enormous Baby
The Giant	The Ghost	The Hermit
The Bionic Man	The Skateboarder	The Ugly Sister
Hamburger Hog	The Very Thin Person	The Fire-eater
The Slob	The Cop	The Clown
The Surfer	The Beautiful Princess	The Witch

Poems About Paintings

I think kids should know a little about art history, know the names of some of the great artists. So I have kids looking closely at art reproductions partly because it's a good thing to do in itself, and partly because it's a great language stimulus. Students often respond well to something that is there in front of them, whether it's a shell or driftwood, or a painting. The energy field that comes into play between them and the object gets them out of their heads and prompts creativity.

I recommend you gather enough prints for everyone to be able to choose. So for the average class of 30+ students you need at least 50 prints. Van Gogh appeals to everyone. Students also respond well to Brueghel, Chagall, the Impressionists, Goya, Leonardo da Vinci, Gauguin, early Picasso, Paul Klee, Turner, Winslow Homer, Magritte and Escher. "Olga's Galleries" is a rich internet source.

There are many ways to write about paintings (Technically known as ekphrastic poetry). Here are four:

1. Walk into the picture and write about what you experience – using all of your senses.
2. Write a dialogue between things or people in the picture.
3. Use the picture as a starting point for a dream or fantasy poem.
4. Look at a painting with lots of people in it. Choose someone and write a poem in which he or she speaks. Trying to hear his or her voice in your head. Maybe your character is secretly in love with another character in the painting, or just have a quarrel, or is afraid of someone there.

Here's a 6th grader's response to Monet's "Impression, Rising Sun". The painting is a study in muted reds – a deep crimson sun reflected on a river. Interestingly, the student saw the painting as an image of war's aftermath:

The Trip Home

After the war the people who survived came home
the worst feeling
Not even knowing which houses is theirs since their homes
were all burnt
coming home, the worst feeling
finding photos of loved ones you will never see again
coming home, the worst feeling
Looking for a home you will never see again.
coming home, the worst feeling

-Thea Zimmer, 6th grade

Here's a 5th grader's playful response to a Hieronymus Bosch painting:

Jittery Dance

It was
a
jittery jumpy
dance the night
the skeletons came.
They hooted
and hollered
and dances with ease.
They beat
the tables
and shattered
the glasses.
For
it was a
jittery jumpy
dance the night
the skeletons came.

-Aaron Haffner, 5th grade

Here's a touching 8th grader's poem about van Gogh's painting, "The Old Peasant Woman":

Looking at a Lined Face
She's an old peasant woman.
She's had to struggle
laboring in the fields
sowing the seeds
and harvesting the crops out there in the hot sunlight
long winds and harsh rains.

Her children have all left home
her husband died
of too much work and suffering

Her strength is gone.
She has some regrets
but it is all the years of hardship
that write the sadness
in her eyes
– Andrea Baum

Riddles

(Full disclosure – I am a professional riddler. You can find packs of my riddles for sale at www.pomegranate.com. I also have two riddle books on Amazon – "Man without Bones" and "Where the dance begins".)

In the old days everyone – kids, teenagers and adults – used to love telling one another riddles. Riddles are usually quite short. Riddle subjects are always familiar to everyone. The clues are fair but tricky. The best riddles also work as poems.

I introduce them:

"We're going to listen to some riddles and see if we can solve them, then we're going to write our own."

In this kind of riddle something speaks without naming itself, like this rhyming footprints riddle:

> **I show the world that you were here**
> **Sometimes I'm hard to see**
> **sometimes I'm clear**
> **I show your skip, your jump, your run**
> **and when the rain descends**
> **I'm quickly gone.**

The next 2 riddles use metaphor:

> **Strange it is**
> **that I have no tail or head**
> **strange it is**
> **that I have no legs**
> **that I pull on my hot yellow robe**
> **dive between two soft pillows**
> **and disappear into the dark red cave**
> *(answer: hot dog)*

My body is long
my head is a clump of stiff strong stalks
Every morning
and every evening
I wear a soft hat
I enter the cave
and dance across white stones
making them sparkle.
(answer: toothbrush)

Some of them rhyme, some use metaphor, and some use repetition, as in this one:

I am a man without bones
my flesh is white
I am a man without blood
my flesh is cold
I am a man without life
my flesh is shrinking
I am the man
you made and lost.
(answer: snowman)

This traditional riddle uses word-blends, or "kennings":

Four long ground-standers
Four short down-hangers
Two crookers
Two lookabouts
One whiskabout
And a bellowbox
(answer: cow)

Long have I wandered
The wide ways of the whale
And the wild wind.
Storm stirred me
Calm caressed me
The sun and moon
Spread gold and silver
Across my glossy back.

Now the wanderer's
Long salt song
Is near complete.
Here at my quest's end
I tilt tall, break and tumble
White slide hissing at your hopping feet.
(answer: ocean wave)

I continue…

"Let's try writing a riddle together. Clues should be fair but tricky. If you were going to write a riddle about a clock, and you write: **I go tick-tock**, then you've made it too easy. But if you say something like:

I have a face
But no mouth
I have a face
But no eyes
I have hands
But no fingers…

…then you're creating a mystery. So, someone give us a subject – something ordinary, familiar – and we'll make up a riddle about it…"

Possible Riddle Subjects:

Now it's time for you to write your own!

Dog	Navel	Umbrella	Tattoo
Sandcastle	River	Locker	Basketball
Baseball mitt	Volcano	Mirror	Eagle
Fairy	Ashes	Mermaid	Backpack
Fountain	Wig	Spaghetti	Hair-dryer
Match	Earwig	Rainbow	Harp
Memory	Cross	Rumor	Eraser
Doll	Frost	Phoenix	Alphabet
Soap	Whale	Comb	Curtain
Eyelid	Hamburger	Bomb	Bee
Fingerprint	Bike	Pencil sharpener	Stapler
Juggler	Cave	Stomach	Fan
Shoe	Glasses	Teeth	Snake
See-saw	Numbers	Nails	Sponge
Circle	Box	Lullaby	Sleeve
Eye	Egg	Diaper	Firework

Here are more riddles for you to use:

I know no words and yet you speak to me
I know no music and yet you sing to me
I am a stranger and yet you love me.
(answer: baby)

Tower of brick
With a hole from the base
To the crown.
The thin man in gray goes up
The fat man in red comes down
(answer: chimney)

I am made firm
by what you breathe.
I will be with you on your journeys
until I go bald
and retire.
(answer: tire)

We dance between your dancing hands
The soft ball shrinks, the pattern grows.
Blood we give and blood we take.
We dance among the dancing boughs.
(answer: needles)

My skin is made of bone
My hands can grip you tight
I have two eyes
I have no head
I travel left or right
(answer: crab)

Giant bird am I
Though not born from any egg
and feathers have I none.
You see me standing on one leg
tall above the town.
Many nests I work to build
Not one of them is mine.
(answer: crane)

Four little wheels
go round and round
a-rittle and a-rattling
over the ground.
Clatter past the cat-food
zipping past the grains
then come back and
do it all again.
(answer: shopping cart)

Why walk or run when you can hop it
I keep the future in my pocket
(answer: kangaroo)

Scream Poems

In my experience, scream poems work best with middle and high school students.

"We are all living in two worlds – the inner and the outer worlds. As I speak you may be listening to me and at the same time thinking about a row you had with your mom or dad or brother or sister this morning, or a new skateboard trick you're learning. Poetry is a way to build a bridge between these two worlds. Notice how this scream poem I'm going to read to you uses concrete images taken from the outer, physical world – silk, red smoke, metal men, lions – express inner feelings. A scream is the expression of an intense feeling. This feeling can be positive or negative. When a woman is having a baby for example she may scream... some of the scream may be through pain, but some of it will be relief, maybe, or joy."

Here's a list of possible screams:

The scream of fear	The scream of love	The scream of birth
The scream of anger	The scream of joy	The scream of pain
The crazy scream	The scream of life	The scream of excitement
The scream of discovery	The scream of loneliness	The scream of frustration
The scream of victory	The scream of loss	The scream of want

"Let yourself go with this one. If anger spills out on to the page, let it happen. If what you write is too raw or personal to show anyone, that's fine. It's yours. You decide if you want to share it or not."

Here are some examples:

> **So many years living with the urge to scream**
> **I held it in so long that it gave birth to three giants.**
> **It felt like silk wrapped tight around me.**
> **It felt like red smoke**
> **flying out of my mouth.**
>
> **Lions were roaring**
> **and an army of metal men**
> **marched out the door**
> **and away down the street.**
>
> **Police car sirens.**
> **Howling dogs.**
>
> **Late in the night**
> **I opened the window**
> **and in the quiet**
> **I heard someone**
> **a long way away**
> **screaming.**
>
> \-   Anonymous

I usually display a big print of Munch's Scream painting.

'Think about the scream you want to write about. As you think about it check out these questions which might help you find concrete images that will make your scream real."

- What shape is this scream?
- If you could touch it, what would it feel like?
- What kind of weather would it be?
- What kind of music would it be?
- Where or what is its home?
- What animal would it be?

Here are 2 scream poems by 10th graders:

The Scream of Joy
I have to let it out
the burning desire to scream

a scream that will tell the world
how happy I am

I will scream in the middle of a crowd
I will scream for the summer and the family

I will scream for the river and the rocks
the food and the noisy kitchen

my scream will be yellow
like the sun rays bursting through the forest

it will be the sound of kids playing
the sound of a blue jay screeching

it's the happiest scream
the world will ever hear

the scream of a girl
about to live her dream!
- Paige Farrell

<u>Voice</u>
The man sits alone
utterly alone
no one around
no one to care.

He starts to whisper
no one hears
he begins to talk
but no one answers
he starts to sing
but
when no one harmonizes
he realizes
he is alone with his voice

he stands up yelling
hoping to prove a point
if I go loud enough
someone will come

he screams
he screams his very own scream
day after day
screaming
but no one notices

it goes out
goes silent
stops
like a light
an unheard voice
never known
for he screams to be heard
but no one answered
he screamed to exist
but no one would vouch for him
what is voice when no one can hear it?
– Julia Neal

Skinny Poems

Students enjoy skinny poems. It's a form that enables them to finish a poem quickly, and it's unfamiliar. It helps if you choose a subject that will work for a skinny poem...a skinny poem about a mouse is more likely to work than a skinny poem about an elephant. (Although, of course, there are no guarantees in poetry.) Keep lines really short – maybe 4 words max.

Here is one by me:

Rain
almost silently
countless drops
of rain
are falling in
wide soft masses
but separately
through
the air
through
cool gray space
until they land
plip
plop
splat
splash
and find
their way
back together again.

Here's a poignant skinny poem by a 5th grade girl:

Peace
so little
but so huge
remembered then
forgotten again

anger moves
I'm gone
quickly as I
come

Keep me
save me

In the dark
I am light
impossible to keep
impossible to have
never there
but never gone

– Mara MacLean, 5th grade

We often complete this project by writing finished skinny poems in big clear writing (having checked and edited them first) on long thin strips of card, with a design or picture on the other side, which we then hang from the ceiling as mobiles.

Possible skinny poem subjects:

Clouds	Cat	Mouse	Bird
Ice	Snow	Tree	Flower
Baby	Music	Moon	Stars
Wind	Dreams	Sleep	Tears
Snake	Bee	Butterfly	Eyes
Hunger	Love	Music	Smile

Surreal Poems

I think you, as the teacher, have to decide if you're comfortable with this kind of poetry before you teach it. (This applies to all the ideas in this book of course.) If you don't 'get' surrealism then it's probably best to leave it alone. When it works, however, a surrealist poetry session can be exhilarating.

Materials:

If you can, bring in paintings by surrealists like Magritte, Dali, de Chirico, Max Ernst etc. There are plenty of examples on the web.(See "Olga's Galleries"). Magritte is always popular. And if you decide to do surreal collages you'll need old newspapers and magazines, glue, scissors and paper.

I introduce it:

"We all have dreams, so we're all familiar with crazy things happening in crazy ways. You might have dreamt about dancing with a vacuum cleaner, or speaking poems to a cement mixer and watching it lay them out on the sidewalk for all to see. You might have had a flying dream, or a dream in which people had hats on the front of their heads and their faces on the top. Some artists and writers explore this crazy dream world in paintings and writing. This dream-like art is called surrealism."

Here's a surreal poem:

Number Thirty-three

Down the shiny orange street
a man is running.
There's a long rope attached to his belt
on the other end is a bronze statue of a giraffe.
Three eyes are watching him
the eye of a storm
the eye of an empty gun
the eye of a one-eyed ticket inspector.

The man runs past number twenty-five.
The man runs past number twenty-seven.
Number twenty-nine has fallen into the sea.
Number thirty-one is an abandoned warehouse
full of plastic dolls crying 'Mama'.
The man takes a chicken out of his pocket
and throws it in the air.
It turns into a pineapple
sprouts a pair of wings
and flies away.

Number thirty-three is the man's home.
The man unlocks the door and walks in.
Everything is as it was twenty years ago.
The man unlocks a cupboard.
He pulls out a sunlit meadow.
The man lies down
in the long grass
and goes to sleep.
The eyes close.
- E.W.

Warm-ups:

(If you think your students are ready to write surreal poems, don't bother with the warm-ups.)

1. Here's a pile of old magazines, plus there are scissors, glue-sticks and plain paper...I want you to create crazy collages...working individually or in small groups. Cut pictures out and re-arrange them. A man with a car for a head, for example; an elephant or a great white shark with a belly full of politicians' faces. If you like you can write poems based on the collage images.

2. We're going to play a game called Exquisite Corpse. Get into groups of 3 or 4. One of you writes a sentence at the top of the page, and then folds the paper so that only part of what you wrote can be seen. You pass the paper to the next person who writes something that includes and adds to what you wrote. Person 2, in the same way as person 1, hides most of what they wrote and passes the paper on to no. 3. And so on. You keep going until the page is full. Then you unfold the page and read what you all wrote.

Here's a surreal poem in dialogue form:

The Man in the Black Suit
I know all about your secret messages
said the man in the black suit
and I know all about your high jumps
and your internal combustions
and your fly-by-nighters
and your fifty-seven famous ways of saying Yes.
No point in thinking you can get away with that kind of
folderol

not while I'm in the neighborhood
Sonny Boy Blue!

Actually I said my name's not...

AND

said the man in the black suit
I know all about your yellow nicknames
and about your lullaby for dead chimneypots
oh yes don't you worry about that
and all the silver steeples you've been chasing
down among the parrot sticks in Dead Man's Holy Gulch.
You and your white Polaroids
you and your bagpipe trousers
you and your tubes...
Oh yes I've had my eye on you for some time now
Mr. Legs in Liquorice

Actually I said my name's not...
Don't interrupt he said.
Have an almond
-   E.W.

You can write a surrealistic description of a place. You could for
example have an agent showing prospective tenants around a house
(the house is a symbol of the self, by the way).

Here's a surreal house poem by an 10th grader from the UK:

Warped Glass

Quietly I enter the house
so as to awake no one
tiptoeing up the banisters
and entering the hall
taking care to avoid the dog
with its electric tail and submarine drooling.
In the attic an empty rocking chair
swings backwards and forwards backwards and forwards
backwards and
while down below Grandad whittles
spilling blood from innocent wood.
In the schoolroom young Jonah
playfully slaps his teacher for being late
and Mother sings old Beatles songs to a sleeping lobster
nestled in the swaying crib.
The clock was humming manically fast in the basement
until Father threw it in the washing machine.
Meanwhile Marilyn rearranged the molecules in the kitchen
and a large mirror was cracking under the strain
allowing shards of warped glass to fall to the ceiling.

Possible surreal writing themes or first lines:

The machine

When the clocks struck midnight

Finally he opened the door

The camel sat opposite him and smiled

The enormous chicken

The runaway snowman

Welcome to our party

She had the unicorn dream again

The whale was very sad

The artichokes were out in the fields planting rows of Barbie's

The message in the bottle

The robot

"Teach Me" Poems

(Inspiration for this idea comes from Carol S. Peck's chapter "Prayers for the Earth", in an excellent book: <u>The Alphabet of Trees, A Guide to Nature Writing</u>, ed. by Christian McEwan and Mark Statman, pub. by Teachers and Writers Collaborative, New York.)

Some people think human beings are higher than animals and plants and things like rocks and water. This way of seeing is called The Great Chain of Being, It's like a ladder, and we humans are at the top. Other people – Native Americans for example – see everything, all forms of life as being on the same level as us on what's called The Great Wheel of Life.

<u>This Netsilik poem offers an interesting slant:</u>

> **In the very earliest time,**
> **when both people and animals lived on earth,**
> **a person could become an animal if he wanted to**
> **and an animal could become a human being.**
> **Sometimes they were people**
> **and sometimes animals**
> **and there was no difference.**
> **All spoke the same language.**

According the Great Wheel view of life, animals and other life forms can teach us useful lessons. In "Teach me" poems we ask them to do this.

Writing "Teach me" Poems

"This is a 'you' poem. You're talking to an animal, or a plant or whatever that can do something you'd like to do, and you're asking it to teach you this quality or skill. When you think about it, pretty well everything can teach us something. A school desk can teach me patience, or the willingness to be a support to others. A school locker can teach me to be a trustworthy friend, one who keeps a secret. A door can teach me when to open my heart to someone and when to keep it closed. A window can teach me to look into other dimensions, to look out when I'm in, to look in when I'm out, or to let the light into my world. A blade of grass can teach me to sway with the wind."

This "teach me" idea may go beyond the animal kingdom, as in this fine poem by New Mexico poet Nancy Wood:

Prayer to the Earth
Earth teach me stillness
As the grasses are stilled with light.
Earth teach me suffering
As old stones suffer with memory.
Earth teach me humility
As blossoms are humbled with beginning.
Earth teach me caring
As the mother who secures her young
Earth teach me courage
As the tree which stands alone.
Earth teach me limitation
As the ant who crawls on the ground.
Earth teach me freedom
As the eagle who soars in the sky.
Earth teach me resignation
As the leaves which die in the fall.
Earth teach me regeneration
As the seed which rises in the spring.
Earth teach me to forget myself
As melted snow forgets its life.
Earth teach me to remember kindness
As dry fields weep with rain.

I read some Teach me poems, then they write their own.

<u>Here's a poem by a 5th grader:</u>

<u>**Teach Me**</u>
Oh deer
Teach me to be graceful and run with the wind
Teach me to gallop so softly
I feel like I can fly so high in the sky
Oh humming bird

Teach me to take people from place to place so we can be united
Teach me to gather pollen from one flower to another
So that the flowers can grow tall

Oh tree
Grow so big that I can climb you and all my worries will be gone
Teach me so I can sway with you in your branches
When the wind comes I can feel the soft gentle breeze on my Face

Oh creek
Teach me to be calm like you are in different areas
Teach me to be still so I can see I am a good person inside

Oh wild penguins
Teach me to waddle with you and slide with my friends so I can have fun
Teach me to climb a mountain and help me so I will not fall or give up

Because you are my best friends forever.
-Aase Mitchell, 5th grade

Here is another:

Wolf

Teach me oh wolf
How to sniff the smallest wind
For storms and stories

Teach me to read the language
Of grasses and leaves
So that I may know
When danger is near.

Teach me to howl
So that I may find my pack
And not be alone.

- E.W.

Here is a list of possible "teachers":

Elephant	Cat	Snake	Dolphin
Crab	Ant	Spider	Squirrel
Stork	Swan	Camel	Grasshopper
Parrot	Butterfly	Worm	Lion
Crocodile	Panther	Pelican	Shark
Songbird	Tree	Reed	Rose
Onion	Lily	Willow	Pinecone
Roots	Ivy	Stars	Clouds
Frost	Ocean	Blood	Moon
Time	Stone	Light	Echo

<u>Ways of Looking</u>

(See notes for "Transformations" in the oral section.)

The prime poetic example of this technique is "Thirteen ways of looking at a blackbird", by Wallace Stevens.

The best results I've had with this exercise come from students working with objects: shells, driftwood, fruit, bones, stones, small tools, candles, screws, bits of rope, etc. Enough for each student to have one, with some to spare. Sometimes students elect to work in pairs.

The art movement known as Cubism was an exploration of ways of looking. To quote from Wikipedia "...*instead of depicting objects from one viewpoint, the artist depicts the subject from a multitude of viewpoints...*"

"Which is my real hand?" you might ask, holding it flat with the palm towards the students, then turning it so it's an edge, then curling it into a fist, pointing it downwards with fingers splayed. It's the shape of a gun, it's a hole like a seashell, it's a four-legged, one-clawed crab. The right brain plays, remember. It dances about. It transforms the familiar. It sidesteps identity and says, *"Look what we have here!"* It accepts no single point-of-view as the "right" one, the "official" one. It shifts the angle, comes close and zooms away.

<u>I say to the class:</u>

"When you write a "Ways of Looking" poem you write a series of short poems each one of which is about the same thing, but looking at it from a different viewpoint. It's a bit like changing camera angles in a film. You can pick an object from one of the bags to write about, or you can choose a word from the list. Remember one of the ways of varying the point of view is to write an "I" poem, a "You" poem or an "It" poem."

"If you choose an object, sit with it for a while, looking at it from different angles, closing your eyes maybe and touching it with your fingertips...wait for the ideas it gives you..."

Here's one by two 5th grade girls:

Five Ways of Looking at a Limpet Shell

1.

Whoever built that teepee over there

forgot to put in a door

2.

The great white mountain

rises to a peak

on the far side

of the golden desert.

Do not come too near.

It may be a volcano.

3.

Hey little Wiz!

You lost your hat again!

4.

I am the point of a bullet

fired from a snowman's gun.

5.

This is the where the eye lived

before it went blind

<u>Here is another example:</u>

<u>Five Ways of Looking at Eyes</u>

1.

What this eye sees

is what that eye misses.

2.

If I look at you with open eyes

I see you.

If I close my eyes

I still see you.

Which one is real?

3.

When your eyes turn away

from the suffering of others

angels weep.

4.

The eye does not know

what 'blue' is

but the sky

makes it happy.

5.

In the eye of the dictator

everyone is an enemy.

In the eye of the killer

everyone is a victim.

In the eye of the saint

everyone is forgiven.

- E.W.

<u>I continue with the class:</u>

"If you choose a word, one way to get started is to create a cluster. Write the word in the middle of your page with a line around it, then write other words that occur to you or that it suggests to you in a circle around your key word. Put a line around each of them, and a line connecting them to the key word. When your cluster is finished you should have a whole lot of ideas to write about. Another way into this is to write your word then write a word association list."

If you want to do a Ways of Looking class poem, (and this is often a good idea, especially with younger students) I suggest you choose a familiar classroom object. The magic of the creative right brain is clearly seen when it takes something ordinary and plays with it. "Ways of looking at a pair of scissors…" "Ways of looking at a stapler…" Encourage the students to bypass the simile structure ("It's like…") and go straight into the transformations.

A session outside the classroom led to this 3rd grade group poem:

8 Ways of Looking at Trees
A tree is a hall where the birds put on a concert every day
A tree is a wrinkled old man with wicked intent
Scratching at windows ands scaring babies
A tree is a lady in a new coat in spring
And nothing in winter because she wanted too much
Some trees are nonconformist, but not very many
A tree is a house where you don't have to pay rent
A tree is a place to hide when you want to sulk
Where they can't find you
A tree is like an old friend – it grows on you.

Ideas for "Ways of Looking" Poems:

Me	Night	Storm	Clouds
Volcanoes	School	Hands	Stars
Red	God	Dogs	Nights
Milk	Scream	Spring	Laughter
Ocean	Death	Childhood	School
Skin	Eyes	Poetry	Memories
Time	Home	Sleep	Love
Sleep	Candle	Baby	Bird
Sky	Water	Garden	Wind

What-ifs

"When she was a kid in England my daughter would make up stories and plays with her friends in our back garden. They inspired me to write these "What-ifs". I'd like to read them to you...but I'd like someone to read with me. I read a what-if, the student reads a what-if, and so on. Any volunteers? Great! Thanks! Here we go."

The What-if Game
What if there was a tree that had such long roots that they went right through the center of the earth and grew another tree on the other side of the world...
What if helicopters cut circles in the air and they went spinning across the sky like see-through flying saucers...
What if people got their hands stuck in their pockets and couldn't get them out again...
What if sunsets were musical...
What if cheese moooed at night...
What if every light bulb had a name and when you say it the light goes on...
What if your mouth closed tight every time you tried to eat junk food...
What if all the dead people came back to life and joined hands and made a circle all around the equator...
What if people's knee-caps fell in love with other people's knee-caps...
What if number seven disappeared...
What if you could unscrew any part of your body that wasn't working properly and trade it in for a new one...
What if students got paid for coming to school...
What if cell phones started texting one another...
What if someone found out that life is a video game...
What if people sang everything, and never spoke....
What if all the cabbages in the world exploded at the same time ...

"Ok... now try writing your own What-ifs. You can work together."

Writing About People

Visualizing someone – warm up:

"I'd like you to look carefully at me, really carefully, then close your eyes and remember what I look like, with as much detail as possible. Color of eyes...shape of my face, shape of my mouth, clothes, everything. Then open your eyes and see how accurately you remembered what I look like. If you didn't do as well as you'd like to, try again.

Now...close your eyes again, and visualize someone in your family. It's up to you who it is. Could be your mom, your dad, a brother or sister. See this person as clearly as you saw me...not just what they look like, but how they walk, their smile, the sound of their voice, the feel of their hand in yours maybe...Now I'm going to stop talking and give you some time to visualize this person in your head..."

(If you think your students don't need the next exercise don't bother with it.)

"Now we're going to create a person. I'm going to ask you questions and write the answers on the whiteboard, (or the OP or the computer...whatever works.) Ready? Here we go.

Is this person male or female?
Female. Okay.
Is she young, middle-aged or old?
Young. Okay. In her teens? Yes?
So we're thinking about a teenage girl...
Tall, average, short?"
So you go on...

"Color of hair, eyes...clothes, style...the objects in her purse...Can you hear her laugh? Can you hear her voice when she's embarrassed or uncertain.

Eventually you get to maybe the biggest step:

"Name?"

"Natalie."

"Okay...let's write a poem about Natalie as though she's speaking. Where is she? Is she in her room?"

I bought an old copy of "The Family of Man" and cut out dozens of black and white photos of people backed them with card and have them on hand for this Writing about People exercise. Also paintings of people: portraits or self-portraits, kids playing, etc. I think it's good to have a choice of physical stimuli in the classroom.

In right brain work you can choose the point of view. So if you're writing a poem about a person you can write as though the person is speaking – an "I" poem, or as though you're talking to the person – a "You" poem, or about the person, a "He" or "She" poem. "I" poetry is the closest, because you're identifying with the person; "You" poems are a little more distant; and "He" or "She" poems the most distant.

Here's an example of a People Description poem written by a 6th grade student:

Old Lady
You usually help me across the street.
You have a great heart.
I wish I could be like you again,
young and beautiful.
I wobble and I'm wrinkled.
I walk slow and I talk slow.
I wish I could drive
and run like you.
Thanks for helping me.
Thanks for having a great heart.

Here is one of mine. I wrote this poem as though a baby was talking to the father he/she rarely sees:

Daddy

Sometimes you tell me you love me

love me

So why don't you want to be near me

near me

You come home from work and you turn on the TV

TV

Daddy

Sometimes you smile and hold me

hold me

You pull funny faces and tell me a story

story

But most days I cry 'cos you don't want to see me

hear me

Daddy

If it's my fault would you tell me

tell me

I just want us to be happy

happy

So please make some room in your heart for your baby

baby

love me

baby

Daddy

Yellow Bird Gallery

This is a popular activity, especially with teens.

Sample poem for Yellow Bird Gallery:

Let's face it she whispered
gazing from behind the mirror
at lost hashtags galloping about
between the hills
I thought you were a lost snowman
I saw the red flowers trembling
at the memories of fire
but now and here in the here and now
all that's left
is the rain in the window
and tall trees swaying beyond the second gate.

Words for Yellow Bird Gallery Word Cards can be found on page 199 at the back of the book. Scan and print these word groups, mount them on thin card, and cut them up so that they're separate.

Instructions to the class:

"Lay these cards on your desk facing upwards and put them together to make lines of poetry. You can add any words that you need."

SECTION FIVE

Enrichment Activities

Enrichment Activities

Guided Imagery

"I'm going to give you a scene to see in your head, to visualize. Put your arms on your desk and rest your head on your arms. Make yourself as comfortable as you can. Now relax...relax the whole of your body from your feet upwards. Take some deep breaths. Good...now stay with what I'm saying, try to stay focused on it."

Visualization #1

You're standing in the back garden of a big house. It's a sunny day and you can feel the warmth of the brick wall you're leaning against passing through your clothes into your body. You close your eyes and listen to the breeze quietly rustling the trees at the end of the garden. Small birds are singing and you can hear the shouts and screams of children playing in the park at the end of the road. From somewhere in the house behind you comes the sound of music... maybe someone's playing the piano, or watching TV.

Out of a pet flap in the back door to your right comes a dog. You can see how big it is, this dog, what color it is, how long its hair is, its tail and so on. The dog sniffs the air, sees you and runs along the path at the back of the house towards you. You crouch down and give the dog a hug. It licks your face and wags its tail and gives a little whine of appreciation. Then it's off, running in crazy circles around the lawn like a toy engine on a circular track...round and round it goes as though in love with running. Then it lies on its back with its paws and hairy legs pointing at the sky and rubs its spine from side to side against the warm short grass as though scratching an itch. It makes you smile to see it. Then it's up and away through the flower beds into the shadowy areas at the end of the garden. You can see the lower branches of bushes shaking as it charges around, barking excitedly, digging for bones it buried or old tennis balls. Above it birds and squirrels are scolding it as it charges around in what they see as their territory, but of course it takes no notice.

The dog's energy and joy lift your heart and you smile as you watch it. An airliner crosses through the sky miles above you, and you think of the people in its long and sleek body sitting in rows, maybe sleeping or listening to music or watching a movie. It feels good to be where you are. The dog comes dashing back across the lawn to you, bits of twig and leaf sticking to its tongue. You crouch to give it another hug, and you smell its warm doggy smells. It licks your hand, runs along the path back to the door, crawls in and through the flap, probably in search of a cold drink. You stand there for a while, watching the birds return to their trees, hearing the kids in the park at the end of the street. Then you walk back along the path and go into the house.

Visualization #2

It's a beautiful sunny day. You and your family are having a picnic on the beach. Everyone is relaxed and happy, and the food tastes good out in the open air. After lunch everybody sits back in their beach chairs or lies on a blanket to relax and sunbathe. You feel like going for a walk, so you cross the sand to the edge of the sea and stand there for a while feeling the cool breeze on your face and looking at the foam left by the waves, seeing the sparkle of it in the sunlight. You remember a cave you found when you were here before, over there at the foot of the cliffs at the far end of the beach. You look back, wave to your family, and walk along the edge of the sea towards the cliff, keeping an eye out for big waves. There are pelicans out there above the ocean, floating around on their broad wings, sometimes tilting forwards, folding their wings and diving into the sea, hitting the water with a big splash, then flying back up to try again. Soon you are close to the cliffs. The waves are crashing against the rocks at its base. You climb over a big rock and slide down the other side.

The cave is still there. You stoop a little and walk into it. It's deeper than you remember, and it slopes towards the back. You go down in your hands and knees and crawl into the darkness. At the back of the cave you see a white shape. As you come closer you realize it's a seagull. It squawks at you and flaps one of its wings. You see fishing line tangled around its legs and its wings. It looks as though it hurts the gull when it moves. You take off your jacket, pass it over the gull's head and body, and wrap the bird up so that it can't move. You feel in your pocket and take out your nail clippers. Holding the bird with one hand and arm, you move to the side slightly so that more light is shining in from the front of the cave. Then very carefully, you reach down with the nail clippers and start snipping the line wherever you can without hurting the bird. The seagull calms down a little as though it realizes it can't escape. You're talking quietly to it. Soon you are able to pull at the line and disentangle the bird. One leg is free, then the other, and then its wing is free. As carefully as you can you crawl towards the front of the cave on your knees and elbows holding the bird in your jacket as though it were a precious parcel. When you come out of the cave the sunlight seems stronger than before and the sound of the waves seems louder. Slowly you open the jacket. You feel an electric thrust as the seagull opens it big wings and springs towards the sky. It finds a flow of air on the cliff face and rises on it, widening and flapping its wings as though beating out the kinks. Then it swoops away across the sea squawking at the sky, rising up and down in space as though celebrating its freedom. You watch it as it flies around the headland, and then it's gone. You take a deep breath and say goodbye.

Visualization #3

You're walking along a busy street. There seem to be lots and lots of people out today, and everyone is hurrying along the sidewalk as though on urgent business. Sometimes you get pushed about so much you step into a doorway or the entrance to a shop just to get out of the way. Then someone looks at you closely and smiles. It's a middle-aged woman with short blond hair, glasses, a dark blue jacket and blue jeans. You have no idea who she is or why she's smiling at you. "Hello!" She says your name. "It's good to see you!" You smile uncertainly and walk on along the crowded sidewalk. You look back and there she is, waving at you and smiling. A couple of teenage boys stop and give you high fives. "Hey dude!" You have no idea who they are, but you smile at them. As you walk along more and more people are greeting you and smiling and saying your name, and soon a crowd of people is standing around you reaching out to touch you and smiling at you. You feel like a celebrity. You have no idea what's going on but you're beginning to enjoy it. Soon a couple of big guys lift you up and put you on their shoulders. Now more people can see you, and everyone is cheering and waving. Soon a television crew turns up and you recognize the guy with short white hair who works for CNN. You wave at him and he waves back and the cameras are held high to point at you. The crowd moves along the sidewalk and you float on it as though it were a river. Finally the two guys carry you up the steps to your front door. It opens. Your mom comes out, waving to the crowd and the TV cameras; she gives you a big hug and brings you inside. The front door closes behind you. "What was all that about?!" you say, walking into the kitchen for a glass of water.

Visualization #4

Here's the gate between the path and the road. You open it, pass through, close it behind you and follow the path through the wood. A cold windy day it is, with rain in the air, all the branches above you swaying like crazy dancers. You follow the path downhill past the big gray rock, and here you are on the bank of the lake - the Black Lake as it's called. A few ducks take off as soon as they see you, quacking and rising rapidly into the air. You see a heron watching you from its place in the reeds over on the far side. You walk along the bank to your favorite place, where tree roots, thick and gnarly, make a natural seat above the water. You make yourself comfortable on the thick roots, and look out across the lake. The surface is rippling as the wind blows across it. The big round leaves of water lilies are lifting in the wind and dropping again.

You look down at the surface off the lake. Here it is calm because the wind does not reach it. You lean forward a little. You can see your face looking up at you from the still dark water. As you look, you see a kind of swelling on your forehead. You feel the place with your hand, and yes there's a strange bump there that gets bigger under your fingers. There's no pain, and you feel no alarm, only wonder. You watch your reflection in the water, and see what looks like a horn growing longer and longer, like the horn of a unicorn. It's a creamy gray and has a kind of spiral pattern on it, like a snail shell. Finally the horn stops growing. It's sticking straight out from your forehead, and it's about five inches long. You can see it when you look up. You lean back against the tree, wondering what's going to happen next. Then you feel a kind of soft jolting in the horn, and a ball of brilliant blue light shoots out off the tip off the horn and flies away across the lake. Then it happens again…shoooom…and another ball of brilliant light shoots out from the horn. This time it's bright red. Then another one, green this time. Then an orange one and a yellow one and a white one and a purple one and another blue one and a pink one… one and after another, shooting out of the tip of the horn and flying around the lake as though chasing one another. You see them reflected in the rippling water, and when they come close you hear the musical note that each one of them makes as it passes.

Finally the first blue one crosses to the middle of the lake and hovers there in the wind about three feet above the water. The other globes of brilliant light follow it across the lake to the middle and seem to melt into it so that finally there is only one ball of brilliant blue light left out there. You call to it, and it crosses the lake towards you, hovers in the air in front of you and then reenters the tip of the horn. It's like a soft cool fountain briefly playing in your head. Then the horn shrinks slowly into your forehead and is gone. The wind gusts through the trees and across the water, and suddenly it's cold and raining hard. It's time to go home.

Visualization #5

You're riding along on something – could be a bike, or a scooter, or a skateboard. It's quite early in the morning, and the sidewalk is empty, so you can go pretty fast. You have your helmet on, and you're feeling comfortable and relaxed with your wheels. You turn a corner. The road goes down a long hill that gets steeper and steeper. There's no traffic, no one else around, so you pick up speed as you cruise downhill. Faster and faster you go. The trees and houses on either side turn into a blur of speed. "Wheeeeeeeeeeee!" you yell, crouching a bit to reduce drag.

As you speed faster and faster towards the bottom of the hill you see that the road goes over a small hump-backed bridge that crosses a creek. The bridge looks quite steep, and you wonder how safe you are going to be crossing it at such speed. Even as you're thinking this you're shooting up the near side of the bridge. When you reach the top you're going so fast you take off, and you're flying up and away. Up and up you go, higher and higher. Now the road is way down there beneath you. You're flying over houses, you're flying over trees, you're flying through wisps of damp white cloud, past startled birds and a small gray plane going in the opposite direction. You have no fear. No worries about what's going to happen. You feel quite safe, and you're enjoying the sensation of floating through the air, feeling the cold damp wind on your face.

Finally you begin to lose momentum. You see the shiny gleam of a lake down to your right, and you tilt your weight and bank down towards it. It's in a marshy area, and you clip the tops of high slender reeds as you descend. You skim across the surface of the lake, catch the water like a skier, plane across the surface, and finally sink in and stop near the opposite bank. When you put your feet down you find the lake's quite shallow here, and you walk to the bank quite easily. You climb out, shake some of the water out of your clothes, check your helmet, and ride away on your wheels in search of home. As you leave the lake, you stop for a moment and look back and up at the sky you traveled across. You're thinking no one will ever believe you did this, but that's okay.

Visualization #6

You find yourself awake in the night and wonder as you lie there what it was that woke you up. Some kind of sound was it? You think so. You think you're hearing it now but you're not sure if you're hearing it or remembering it. It's a single note, not low, not high, a sound that's very pure and clear. It reminds you of the sound you get when you rub your finger around the top of a fine wine glass: ooooooooooooooooooooo. On and on it goes. You think it's coming from outside. You open the window. Full moon. Such a peaceful night. Somewhere not far away a dog barks. No urgency, no alarm. It's as though it's barking at a dream. The moonlight shines on flowers and patio furniture and casts deep shadows across the garden. Ooooooooooooooo…the pure clear note goes on and on. When you listen hard, when you concentrate on it, the sound seems to grow louder. It fills your mind so that you find it hard to think about anything else. You lean out of the window and gaze at the moonlit garden. There's something down there. It's alive. It's calling to you.

You put on sneakers and a hoodie, move quietly through the house, out through the back door. The sound's louder now. You wonder if anyone else can hear it. You don't think they can, although you're not sure why. Beyond the fence at the back of your garden is a kind of wild area; there's an old shed and an upside-down boat with holes in it, and an old car with no wheels. You and your friends used to play out there when you were kids, making up stories and plays, inventing new languages and codes, frightening one another with ghost stories. You think this is where the sound is coming from. You open the gates in the back fence and walk quietly into the wild area. Then you stand still for a while, listening. The sound comes back and you answer it ooooooooooooooooooo on the same note. You walk across the wild area to a big hollow tree where you used to have a camp. The sound is coming from inside the hollow tree. You make the sound back to it: ooooooooooooooooooo... it's as though you're having a conversation. Soon you stop, and when you do the sound stops coming from inside the hollow tree. It's coming out, the creature making the sound. You hear it moving in the shadows. Finally you see it. You hold out your hand to touch it. You are the only person in the world who knows what it looks like.

Visualization #7

I'm here on the bank of a river, not far from a bridge, fishing. I'm about nine years old. My dad's along the river to my left somewhere. It's a grey day; there's rain in the air and the bank is squishy under my boots. I can smell the river. I always call it a brown smell. I've put my rod together, fixed on my reel, threaded the line through the rings, slid on my thin red bobber, my hook, the lead weights and the bait, and cast it over the reeds into the current. It floats down the river to the right for a few yards. I pull it in and cast it upstream to my left. Again and again I do this, watching the bobber, hearing the watery ripples, the plip plipping of raindrops, smelling the river, the marshy mud. I feel the tension in me relaxing a bit. Seems like I've been doing this forever… cast, watch the bobber follow the current, reel in, cast it upstream, over and over and over again. Don't give up said my dad, last time we came. And the time before. I think they have an agreement, the fish in this river. Don't take his bait! Pass it on! Don't take his bait! Cast… watch the bobber, reel in…cast. MY BOBBER'S GONE! IT DISAPPEARED. WHERE'S IT GONE? I lift the rod. I've caught a fish! There's a fierce tugging coming up the line. The rod's bending, the fish is pulling, pulling at the line; there's the sense of a living creature tugging, pulling, fighting, a feeling that goes all the way through me, like electricity.

Carefully I reel the line in. There it is, a beautiful silvery fish beating the surface with its tail. I lift it carefully over the reeds and swing it in, and reach out to hold the line between the bobber and the fish.

"Dad!" I shout. "I caught a fish!" He comes running along the bank. He holds the fish carefully and disengages the hook. "Well done!" he says. "It's a beauty." I touch the silvery side of the fish. It's smooth and cold and slightly slimy. I slip it into the keep-net. I feel great.

Visualization #8

There's a soldier peering round the corner of a building. He fires his gun down a deserted street, and from the muzzle of his gun streaks a fizzing rocket that bursts into balls of brilliant light above the asphalt; they float around for a while like dandelion seeds then pop! pop! like foam on the edge of the sea, one after another, leaving small, umbrella-shaped clouds that drift away into the sky. Another soldier is walking along the sidewalk when he steps on a hidden mine. It sets off a screeching yellow ball that whizzes around his head like a crazed parrot and then tilts downwards, hits the road and turns into lots of sparks that fizz around like mad ants than sink into the surface of the street. You see kids coming out of their hiding places in the city, lighting sparklers and dancing around with them in their hands. Teenage boys set off fireworks which explode in towers of blueish smoke; they're laughing and cheering. A big grey tank rumbles round a corner at the end of the street; it swivels its long dark gun barrel and fires a long stream of golden sparks that snap and zip around like dragonflies. A low-flying jet roars over the town, its guns rattling, and the air is full of long streamers made of shiny mylar that join together and lay themselves on the rooftops.

It's as though the angels are dropping a blessing on the world. Everybody comes out of their houses and cheers.

What's Going On?

Some of these are narrative fragments, others are events that are complete in themselves but nevertheless mysterious. Their purpose is to get students creating back-story, or making up what happens next. Great for oral work!

Suggestion #1

The old lady comes to the same bench by the lake two or three times a week, usually when it's sunny. She sits for a while gazing at the water, then takes off her shoes and her coat, puts them neatly on the bench by her purse, then walks down the bank into the lake and stands in water up to her waist. She raises her hands towards the sky and sings in a sweet, surprisingly powerful voice. Then she climbs out, puts her shoes back on, and walks away.

Suggestion #2

Christina has always been frightened of balloons. Even now, in her late teens, if there are balloons around, in bunches or tied to the wall or floating above tables at a party, she goes pale and starts trembling and has to leave.

Suggestion #3

He's absolutely certain he saw them there in the closet under the stairs…a whole family of them: father, mother and three children, sitting down to a meal. He watched them for a while. They didn't seem to be aware of him. He's often gone back and opened the closet door and looked in but he's never seen them again. No one believes him except his little sister Mirabelle who says she sees them over the place.

Suggestion #4

He dreamt there was a metal box buried under the middle of his lawn. Next day he started digging and he found the box. When he opened it there was a flash of brilliant light that almost blinded him. It seemed to come from the box. Then it was gone. He found a piece of folded paper in the box. When he opened it he read the words, "Thank you."

Suggestion #5

Finally they broke open the front door and entered the house. It felt like it had been empty for a long time. In the kitchen there was a pile of leather gloves on the table, all large size. They looked as though they'd never been worn. There were white feathers all over the house.

Suggestion #6

The text message said he should climb to the top of Jackson Hill Friday night in the very early hours of the morning. He must tell no one about where he's going. He should bring sandwiches and water in his backpack, and a spare pair of shoes and any object he can find that's made of gold. He should lie on his back on top of the hill and wait. If nothing happens he should do the same thing a week later.

Suggestion #7

He's hiding in a ditch by the side of a track. The ditch is overgrown with brambles and nettles. It's pouring with rain, and he's soaking wet. He hears shouting and the thumping of horses' hooves. He crouches down as low as he can, so much so that he's sitting in cold water, trying not to tremble. Horsemen are galloping along the track. The man in front is riding a huge white horse. His hair is so pale it seems white. Strangely the rain doesn't seem to be falling on him. He's the King. He looks strong and fierce, one who looks danger in the face and doesn't turn away. As they pass he could reach out and touch the hooves of the King's horse.

"One day," he tells himself, "one day I'll stand and bow to him and his men will take me to the castle and feed and clothe me, and the King will give me a task to perform, something difficult and dangerous. When I'm ready I'll stand and step forward. Until then I will remain hidden."

Suggestion #8

That was a long time ago. I was eight years old. I remember that because he wasn't there for my birthday. He'd already been gone for, oh, two weeks at least. No one knew where he was. No one on the island, and no one over there in Parrot Cove. One morning I found one of his shoes on the beach. That really freaked me out. Then he turned up. Walked in through the front door as we were sitting down for dinner. He looked terrible. We had this agreement, mom and me and my sister Maisie and Granny Catstail, that when he came back we would welcome him and love him and not ask him where he's been or what happened. So that's how it was. After a few days he seemed pretty well the same except I noticed he never went near the horses again.

Suggestion #9

People in the village always said that the old well in the middle of the forest had magical properties. If you're there at the right time and make a wish your wish will be granted. Old Man Nosepickle who lived in a tree house told me that the right time was when you could see the reflection of the moon at the bottom of the well. I went there one night when the moon was full and waited as it climbed up to the top of the sky. It was scary I can tell you, sitting alone in the forest, hearing the sounds of animals and the sounds I thought might be animals. Several times I decided to go home but I really wanted to see the moon at the bottom of the well and make my wish. Trouble was the trees were so thick and so close together they blocked the moon almost completely. Even when the moon was directly overhead all I could see was a tiny little chink of pale light down there, so small I wasn't sure what it was. "Wish I could see the moon down there," I thought.

That was when everything went crazy.

Suggestion #10

They are in a dark place, a tunnel. There's a faint glow coming through crimson walls which are criss-crossed by roots or veins, some thick, some thin. Everything is moist and rather slimy, like the inside of a banana peel. The walls are moving, rippling very slowly.

There are five of them. In the gloomy night they see that they are all naked. They are so shocked they feel no embarrassment.

"What happened?"

"Where are we?"

"How did we get here?"

Someone remembers something.

"There was an accident," she says. "Then everything blew up."

"And here we are," says someone else.

Suggestion #11

Everyone warned him against climbing The Big Tree. It was the giant of the forest. People say its roots reach down to the River of Death, and its peak climbs up past the top of the sky to the place where the future is known. But he was a courageous young man and self-willed, and as soon he was old enough to disobey his parents without punishment he started preparing himself for the great climb.

He began his ascent early one morning before the mists had cleared. By noon he was above the rest of the trees. He thought he heard music floating on the air. It was hot up there. He sat on a branch, drank some water, looked across the forests at the distant mountains. Bright clear sky. No wind. Small white clouds like sheep grazing on a blue field. He took a deep breath and reached for the next branch. It was then that the tree began to move from side to side, gracefully, as though it were dancing.

He noticed as he climbed that he was forgetting things – he couldn't remember his sister's name, or the color of his dog's hair, or who lived in the house next door. He went on climbing, up and up and up.

Suggestion #12

His body armor with its plates and segments, its hinges and fastenings, is in place. Sensor systems are clear and on full alert. It's pitch dark in here but he knows his way around. He crouches, stills himself to listen. He hears the others in the dark, close by him. Wait…wait…silence…then a tiny sound, like a secret clicking, passes from one to the next to the next. It's time. Softly they move through the dark.

Suggestion #13

She'd always lived in the big house on the hill, near the edge of the forest, so she was used to hearing animal sounds in the night. But this was different. This wasn't one animal, or two… this was a lot of animals. She could hear yapping and howling, bellowing, screeching, barking, but mostly she heard the sounds of animals running…the beat of hooves and claws and paws on the earth.

She moved her chair beneath the window in her sloping ceiling, climbed up and out and perched on the roof, something her parents had strictly forbidden her to do.

Hundreds of animals were running through the dark in a great mass, ancient enemies some of them, all running with a single purpose or so it seemed.

Escape.

But from what? No smoke on the wind as far as she could tell, so no fire.

Then she heard a sound so faint and distant it was almost obscured by the drumming of feet and animal voices. It was a roaring sound that was a long way away but that seemed to be getting closer and closer.

Suggestion #14

It started the night she and Steve finally broke up. He always said he loved her but she didn't like how he looked at other girls all the time, and how he flirted when they went clubbing or partying or whatever. Then she caught him making out with Becky Sayles on the stairs at José's birthday party and she screamed at him really loudly so everyone heard, then she slammed out of the house and ran home in the rain. She was in the bathroom cleaning off her makeup and brushing her teeth and she cried for a while 'cause she knew it was over and she really liked him even though she was angry. Then she had to wash her face again 'cause her tears made her all smeary and she was just reaching over to turn off the light when her reflection smiled at her.

Which was weird, because she wasn't smiling.

Suggestion #15

I've never met anyone who knows how Roly Poly began. It's always held the day after the birth of the years' first pupple. Yesterday one was born in Princess Gardens, so today here we are at the bottom of the steepest slope of Hildegard Hill, waiting. I can see Slob up there in his little black loincloth, and Jelly Baby and Wobble, and Blub...plus several new boys in white loin cloths. It's not a race, it's a competition. It's...what they do is...well, I'll just describe it as it happens.

Here's Slob. He's huge. He's up there at the top of the grassy track that descends to the foot of the hill to end on the bank of Big Blue. He's curled himself up into a ball with his head tucked in, and one of the officials rolls him to the top of the track, and then...he's off!

Suggestion #16

On his way home one evening he saw a seashell on the sidewalk. He stopped and picked it up. It was a delicate pink, about the size of his thumbnail, with stripes radiating outwards from its back like late sunlight passing through clouds. He stood on the sidewalk holding it carefully between the tips of his thumb and forefinger. It was exquisite.

The color of the shell, the curve of its edge and the faint ridges he could feel against his skin: all this was taking him back to a place and time he hadn't thought of years, and it was as though he was there, back there, looking at the pink seashell that someone had given him a long time ago. It made him happy. Remembering this made him happy. He smiled, slipped the shell in his pocket and walked home.

Suggestion #17

I've been down here for a long time. I honestly don't recall how it happened. I looked around one day and, well, this is where I found myself.

I talk to myself a lot, since there's no one else to talk to. I do remember how it happened. I just don't want to think about it.

I need to find a way out of here. It shouldn't be too difficult. So I keep telling myself.

This is me, talking to myself again, looking for a way out of here.

Suggestion #18

Last Friday he took a nice long bath in an active volcano, then he went shark-hunting with his bare hands.

Saturday morning he memorized Shakespeare's Midsummer Night's Dream. Saturday afternoon he finished building his rocket and took off for a quick trip around the equator.

Sunday he rested in his hammock at the top of the world's tallest tree.

Monday he talked on the phone for a while and earned 3 1/2 billion dollars. That was in the morning. In the afternoon he discovered a cure for AIDS. Monday evening he sang ten of his own songs with Coldplay as his backup group then flew his helicopter over to Carnegie Hall where he played solo instruments in Rachmaninoff's second piano concerto and Beethoven's Violin Concerto. Yesterday he won Olympic gold medals in the 100 meters sprint, the high jump, and the 200 meter relay swim which he swam alone. Then he went home and wrote his autobiography; by six in the morning it had sold 2 million copies.

This morning he disappeared.

Suggestion #19

Christine said she saw me last week at the pool. "You were doing great!" she said. "I mean your crawl is like to die for…" She put her hand on my forearm is though impressed by my muscles.

"Actually, Christine, I don't…I can't swim."

It was happening again.

"But I saw you there!" she said. "Black trunks…same hair…guitar tattoo on your…"

"Okay, okay!" I said. I walked down the steps out of school and across the car park.

Gina saw me playing chess in a coffee bar in Mill Valley. Sam saw me at a park in San Diego, and her friend Erika saw me in August on a freaking Greek island…sitting with a gorgeous blonde girl in a bar near the beach. Swears it was me. They all swear it was me. They're all girls, which is strange.

Here's the strangest thing though: my girlfriend Miranda says she thought she went with me last night to see a Russell Crowe movie. I'd already told her about people seeing me in all sorts of places, so she kind of knew something was going on.

She said, "The movie was really good Guy…you should see it…"

"So you don't think I have."

"Well, here's the thing…we were in the Motley afterwards having a drink and he reaches across and takes my hand and out of nowhere I'm like: "Who the hell are you?" And he says I'm Guy and I say I don't believe you. Then he looks at me, gives me this really intense look, like he really loves me. Then he says, Tell Guy I'm sorry. And he leaves."

She looked worried. She put her hands on either side of my face and gazed into my eyes. "What's going on?"

Suggestion #20

The report said the night janitor of Brentwood Mall saw an intensely bright light shining through the glass dome above the central sitting area. He was just passing Victoria's Secret and he shone his flashlight at it and the bulb burst. When he tried to use his cell phone, he got an electric shock. Then he must've blacked out. He remembers falling over and reaching for his gun…When he came to it was early morning, and one of the cleaning ladies was shaking him. He stood up. His phone was still fried and his gun was gone. He was okay. The cleaning woman tugged his sleeve and asked him in Spanish to follow her. She led him across the sitting area…benches, a small fountain, palms and ferns in pots. There was a perfect circle, about 12 feet in diameter, cut into the tiled floor. He stooped to look at it. The groove was about half an inch deep. He wondered what could have made it, because the tile was so hard and tough. He put his foot forward into the circle and the cleaning woman cried, "Nada!" and tried to stop him but he shook her off and stepped into the circle. It was as though he had no choice.

Solving Problems

Back in the 70s Edward de Bono, the lateral thinking man, produced a wonderful book entitled "Children solve Problems." I don't believe it's available in the US anymore, although you might be able to get a copy from Amazon UK. He gave children interesting problems to solve, and asked them to draw their machine or invention along with directions as to how it works or how to use it. The results are fascinating. Children came up with wonderful diagrams and highly original and often very detailed ideas.

I've tried this out in classrooms in the US with elementary and middle school students with good results.

Here's how I approach it:

"I'm going to give you three problems to think about. I want you to choose the one you find most interesting and invent a solution of some kind, a machine maybe. I'd like you to draw a diagram of the machine or the invention and write instructions on the diagram. You can work with someone else if you like, and you can do rough draft designs so that you can work out the kinks, the details of how everything functions. The three problems are:

1. A machine for weighing a whale
2. A machine for cleaning the air on smoggy days
3. An instant shelter for homeless people that they can carry around during the day.

Any questions?

Afterwards we'll do a display of them."

Other Possibilities for "Solving Problems":

A machine for catching falling stars

A machine for entertaining bored cats

A machine for catching burglars

A machine that makes time go slower or faster

A machine for building houses out of plastic bottles

A machine for drawing energy from kites

A machine for counting frogs

A machine for helping people sleep

<u>Circles</u>

Take a medium-sized paper plate and use it to draw as many circles as you can on the whiteboard. Have felt pens available.

I say:

"Here's a bunch of circles. 22 of them. I want you to come up, one at a time, take a felt pan and change one of these empty circles into something. The only rule is you can't repeat an idea someone else has already drawn. Any questions? Go!"

Someone will immediately do a face. After this, no more faces. Unless it's a cat's face, or a baboon's, a clock's face, a non-human face. It gets really interesting when all the obvious circle themes are taken. Other possibilities – porthole, telescope lens, eyeball, sleeping cat, crown, frisbee, fish ring on water, rabbit hole…

You can progress from drawn circles on the whiteboard to giving each student a paper plate and freedom to do their own design choosing from a range of materials.

You can use squares, rectangles and triangles in the same way.

APPENDIX I: Words for bag of words

(page 180-198, activity on page 55)

are	are	are	are
are	they	they	they
we	we	no	no
no	yes	yes	yes
yes	because	because	I
I	I	I	I
I	I	Action	ly
ly	ly	ly	ly
battalion	major	key	between
middle	middle	as	under
horizon	blanket	scale	hair
skin	fur	ultramarine	shark
tiger	weather	scoop	crab

curl	puff	pirouette	Snap
bake	flutter	welcome	splash
giggle	murmur	disappear	twist
picture	muscle	hawk	bough
root	shadow	flood	blood
pump	mine	skateboard	my
his	its	its	darling
dungeon	rustle	drive	rose
cross	goodbye	love	cry
laugh	guitar	words	fresh
moon	music	spin	heart
glue	guts	purple	silk
rattle	rock	play	gather
trumpet	cosmos	question	wish

gold	tower	boom	smash
prize	dig	forest	pluck
love	return	circle	blue
stone	cow	squirrel	baby
jet	smile	romance	ache
tumble	move	babble	invite
paint	color	diamond	dream
black	drink	sparkle	moon
blue	silver	cloud	roll
gape	breathe	gulp	boil
scatter	feather	sing	strip
tiny	squash	filter	search
roll	anger	glow	scarlet
dog	satin	cumulus	erupt

seven	space	candle	tape
drive	home	table	ruby
hallo	tank	mysterious	water
cloud	dog	underwater	fray
maiden	gallant	motorcycle	hole
golf	mad	jet	swivel
light	opera	dance	begin
applause	gentle	experiment	crazy
beard	sweat	necklace	wave
shock	mental	basketball	leather
ballet	flute	drum	smallest
green	die	river	pale
detail	forget	and	and
and	you	you	you

but	but	but	and
and	the	the	the
the	first	fire	in
in	in	in	out
out	out	these	these
these	chestnut	tulip	summer
ice	snow	rain	sun
behind	before	between	after
same	bang	swoosh	ing
ing	ing	ing	ing
ing	sus	sus	con
con	pre	pre	pre
dark	set	female	name
pool	pale	gloomy	say

scream	dig	nasty	evil
opposite	jingle	radiant	tinkle
of	of	of	of
ful	ful	ful	ful
ful	ful	power	fool
clown	snake	island	tree
s	s	s	s
s	s	s	s.
s	s	s	s
a	a	a	a
a	a	a	a
a	a	a	a
a	a	a	a
to	to	to	to

an	an	an	an
plastic	dumb	footprint	rub
beetle	creek	savage	god
hero	dragon	sunset	straight
log	drift	bird	gull
sand	tide	feather	grass
bee	honey	century	April
nut	moon	fireworks	fly
rise	tumble	disintegrate	screw
elbow	blade	hamburger	time
flea	navel	highway	cradle
wolf	love	tell	hide
shoot	bang	spring	root
milk	sprinkle	away	distant

walk	butter	monkey	are
are	are	are	they
they	they	we	we
no	no	no	no
yes	yes	yes	yes
because	because	I	I
I	I	I	I
action	ly	ly	ly
ly	ly	ly	ly
battalion	major	between	key
middle	middle	asunder	me
me	me	horizon	sex
scale	skin	blanket	fur
shark	tiger	ultramarine	scoop

weather	crab	curl	puff
snap	bake	pirouette	flutter
welcome	splash	disappear	giggle
murmur	twist	picture	cloud
muscle	hawk	bough	root
shadow	flood	blood	pump
mine	my	skateboard	his
its	its	darling	rustle
dive	rose	dungeon	cross
love	cry	goodbye	laugh
guitar	words	sizzle	thick
the	the	the	the
pink	red	blue	purple
dark	purple	blue	green

green	blue	blue	green
crimson	violet	violet	black
black	black	black	white
white	white	white	silver
silver	silver	rough	smooth
even	gray	gray	gray
brown	brown	brown	egg
orange	orange	speckled	sky
sky	sky	clouds	clouds
clouds	tower	trumpet	sword
dangle	dive	ing	ing
ing	ing	ing	swoon
ripple	horse	tiger	snail
shell	sick	muscle	ride

erupt	swagger	whisper	sway
bump	tumble	swirl	kick
punch	betray	burn	bread
breed	pony	trot	gallop
swirl	kick	punch	betray
burn	breed	pony	trot
gallop	sprint	creep	spring
summer	survival	external	solar
energy	water	fire	earth
air	wind	element	energy
water	fire	earth	air
wind	suspect	element	say
shout	scream	stray	ramble
whistle	deny	future	past

king	queen	ancestor	witch
ring	serpent	stone	fire
light	deep	dig	mix
store	cackle	laugh	candle
flame	scar	girl	boy
storm	trees	foot	love
stars	blue	dreams	etc.
baby	sea	hands	know
door	rain	school	forget
fire	fish	clouds	gold
are	are	are	the
the	the	umbrella	tinkle
drone	hover	hum	solid
huge	hide	flat	miss

rock	squash	turquoise	roll
hard	hold	space	closet
cold	hot	steam	freeze
chase	run	capture	flee
arrest	hide	liberate	ed
ed	ed	ed	ed
ing	ing	ing	ing
ing	ed	fly	clay
wrench	tug	alabaster	pull
squeeze	embrace	bubble	women
lizards	frenzy	surround	shadow
appear	meet	express	choose
time	place	the	the
the	the	this	these

those	weak	strong	flexible
shot	ask	her	her
her	her	him	him
him	him	where	when
when	when	valley	gown
listen	trap	fern	valley
quick	chase	gnash	float
pull	top	backwards	fever
because	bed	forwards	love
fountain	stone	therefore	spring
soft	dog	shepherd	trees
bird	paper	ship	cloud
plane	thank	ask	sink
drown	return	argue	refuse

plead	regret	remember	guess
change	argue	obsess	weep
chase	tell	listen	shake
leg	hand	head	back
finger	chest	eye	sizzle
thick	the	the	the
pink	red	blue	purple
purple	green	green	blue
blue	green	crimson	violet
violet	black	black	black
black	white	white	white
white	silver	silver	silver
rough	smooth	even	gray
gray	gray	brown	brown

brown	egg	speckled	orange
orange	orange	sky	sky
sky	clouds	clouds	clouds
tower	trumpet	sword	dangle
dive	ing	ing	ing
ing	ing	swoon	ripples
horse	tiger	snail	shell
sick	muscle	erupt	swagger
whisper	sway	bump	tumble
swirl	creep	kick	punch
betray	burn	breed	pony
trot	gallop	spring	summer
solar	energy	external	water
fire	earth	air	wind

element	suspect	survival	say
shout	scream	ramble	whistle
deny	future	ancestor	past
king	queen	witch	ring
serpent	stone	fire	light
deep	dig	mix	store
laugh	candle	flame	scar
girl	boy	umbrella	the
the	the	tinkle	drone
hover	hum	shoot	solid
hide	flat	miss	roll
hard	hold	turquoise	space
closet	cold	hot	steam
freeze	chase	capture	liberate

arrest	fly	clay	wrench
tug	pull	alabaster	bubble
women	lizards	surround	frenzy
shadow	appear	meet	express
choose	time	place	the
the	the	this	these
this	those	those	weak
strong	shot	flexible	ask
her	her	her	her
him	him	him	him
where	when	when	when
valley	gown	listen	trot
splash	dark	father	hot
clouds	ice	feather	scald

type	behind	mysterious	dirty
delay	golden	excellent	spray
shimmer	delight	opposite	thunder
crackle	fairy	switch	horses
meadow	taxi	mountains	faint
journey	doubt	sink	gurgle
silly	invade	congrats	dance
son	rock	daughter	roof
goat	swirl	doorway	the
the	the	the	the
the	the	the	the
these	these	these	these
down	down	down	up
up	up	beneath	above

APPENDIX II: Yellow Bird Gallery Word Cards		
(page 199-202, activity on page 154)		
ebb and flow	much too late	silver and gold
the 8th dwarf	nobody left there	fix that puppy
an old man talking	here and there	now and then
in and out	up and down	forwards and backwards
red flowers trembling	the other side	a sweet lie
memories of fire	a sudden silence	who is it?

the next phase	between the hills	a frightened rabbit
Cedric the wolfhound	sarcastic sheep	in the box
look me in the eye	let's face it	how are you?
nice and easy	excitable toes	imagine that
the backwards river	and after that?	between the lines
right or wrong	pink is here	green and tender
go with the flow	galloping about	smaller and smaller

stop it!	birds of panic	here we are
let me see	open your eyes	the enormous cell-phone
fish out of water	the second gate	behind the smile
look what you've done	she whispered	rain at the window
the antelope file	a self-destructive gun	the fifth corner
spinning the wheel	so you say	someone's here
what says the Joker?	behind the mirror	back seat driver

very small elephants	click the button	the lost snowman
trickling blood	another helicopter	he said quietly
they all saw you	news of the goat	the red cauliflower
tall trees swaying	three-way pendulum	the latest
number seven	news of the goat	the lost hashtag

ABOUT THE AUTHOR

Emmanuel Williams has been a teacher for 50 years. He holds a Masters of
Arts in the Teaching of Writing from Humboldt University. He has taught
all over the world, and has worked with students of all ages from second
grade through college. He is a member of California Poets In The Schools,
and has taught poetry writing in the greater San Francisco Bay Area.

His publications include:

Inside Story, and Introductions – two books of ekphrastic poems
about works by English collage artist Sofiah Garrard, published by
Green Chair Gallery, UK
Living in Light – Study of English painter Harold Hitchcock,
published by Phillips Gallery, USA
Loving – truths about sex no one told you
Man Without Bones – original riddles published by Robert Reed
Publications, USA
Old Dog Dreaming – nature poems
Pundit – original puns
Riddle Packs (two decks) – published by Pomegranate Publications,
USA
Singing in the car – poems
There was an old lady from Bristol – original limericks
Where the dance begins – original nature riddles
Witness – Nature poems, Windwords Press, UK

RECOMMENDED READING

Books published by Teachers and Writers Collaborative:

Poetry Everywhere: Teaching Poetry Writing in School and in the Community *by Jack Collom & Sheryl Noethe*

Sing the Sun Up: Creative Writing Ideas from African-American Literature *Edited by Lorenzo Thomas 200 pp*

The Writing Workshop Vols 1 and 2: How to Teach Creative Writing *by Alan Ziegler*

The Alphabet of the Trees: A Guide to Nature Writing *Edited by Christian McEwen & Mark Statman 320 pp*

The List Poem: A Guide to Teaching & Writing Catalog Verse *by Larry Fagin 201 pp*

Others:

A Poetry Handbook *by Mary Oliver*

To Rhyme or Not to Rhyme *by Sandy Brownjohn*

The Practice of Poetry *Edited by Robin Behn and Chase Twichell*

Theater Games for the Classroom *by Viola Spolin*

Made in the USA
San Bernardino, CA
01 August 2017